THEMES
for early years

CONTENTS

THEMES
for early years

CHRISTMAS

LINDA MORT & JANET MORRIS

THEMES
for early years

Authors Linda Mort and Janet Morris
Editor Jane Bishop
Series designer Lynne Joesbury
Designer Glynis Edwards
Illustrations Kim Woolley
Cover Lynne Joesbury
Action Rhymes, Poems and Stories compiled by Jackie Andrews
Songs compiled by Peter Morrell
Assemblies chapter by Lesley Prior

Designed using QuarkXpress
Processed by Scholastic Ltd, Leamington Spa

Published by Scholastic Ltd, Villiers House, Clarendon Avenue, Leamington Spa, Warwickshire CV32 5PR

© 1998 Scholastic Ltd   Text © 1998
1 2 3 4 5 6 7 8 9   8 9 0 1 2 3 4 5 6 7

The publishers gratefully acknowledge permission to reproduce the following copyright material:
Jill Atkins for the retelling of 'Baboushka' © 1998, Jill Atkins, previously unpublished; **Clive Barnwell** for 'The Greatest Gift' and 'There Isn't Any Room' © 1998, Clive Barnwell, previously unpublished; **Ann Bryant** for 'Father Christmas Makes The Toys' © 1998, Ann Bryant, previously unpublished; **Sue Cowling** for 'Wave Your Hands For Christmas' and 'Christmas Cookies' © 1998, Sue Cowling, previously unpublished; **Susan Eames** for 'Santa, Santa' © 1998, Susan Eames, previously unpublished; **Anne Farr** for 'A Busy Time For Mrs Christmas' © 1998, Anne Farr, previously unpublished; **Barbara Garrad** for 'Jesus' © Barbara Garrad, previously unpublished; **Jean Gilbert** for 'Christmas Cheer' © 1998, Jean Gilbert, previously unpublished; **Trevor Harvey** for 'Questions on Christmas Eve' © 1998, Trevor Harvey, previously unpublished; **Penny Kent** for 'Our Christmas Cards' © 1998, Penny Kent, previously unpublished; **Karen King** for 'Mole's Best Christmas' © 1998, Karen King, previously unpublished; **Johanne Levy** for 'Christmas Giving' © 1998, Johanne Levy, previously unpublished; **Wes Magee** for 'The Christmas Tree Lights' and 'A Thinking Christmas' © 1998, Wes Magee, previously unpublished; **Tony Mitton** for 'Christmas Mystery', 'Santa Claus Action Rhyme' and 'Sunny Santa' © 1998, Tony Mitton, previously unpublished; **Peter Morrell** for 'Sharing Christmas' and 'Christmas Pud' © 1998, Peter Morrell, previously unpublished; **Linda Mort and Janet Morris** for 'The Story of St. Nicholas' © 1998, Linda Mort and Janet Morris, previously unpublished; **Judith Nicholls** for 'One, Two, Three' and 'What's In The Parcel' from *Higgledy–Humbug* by Judith Nicholls © 1990, Judith Nicholls (1990, Mary Glasgow Publications); **Sue Nicholls** for 'Paper Chains' © 1998, Sue Nicholls, previously unpublished; **Lesley Prior** for three assemblies © 1998, Lesley Prior, previously unpublished; **Coral Rumble** for 'Busy, Busy Bethlehem' © 1998, Coral Rumble, previously unpublished; **Maureen Warner** for 'Is It Cold At Christmas?' © 1998, Maureen Warner, previously unpublished; **Margaret Willetts** for 'Look At The Baby' © 1998, **Margaret Willetts**, previously unpublished; **Brenda Williams** for 'The Story of the First Christmas' © Brenda Williams 1998, previously unpublished.
British Library Cataloguing-in-Publication Data A catalogue record for this book is available from the British Library.

ISBN 0-590-52726-1

The right of Linda Mort and Janet Morris to be identified as the Authors of this work has been asserted by them in accordance with the Copyright, Designs and Patents Act 1988.

INTRODUCTION

Although Christmas is a once-yearly festival, celebrated by many, but not all people in the world, the spirit of the festival can be maintained and appreciated by everybody throughout the year. The lessons of sharing, giving, cooking together, hospitality, and giving pleasure to one another, which the festival of Christmas so powerfully embodies, are universal experiences, appreciated by everyone the world over.

Through a topic-based focus on Christmas, early years educators can help their children develop skills, attitudes and understanding across the whole early years' curriculum, in ways which are developmentally appropriate for young children in a multicultural world. A topic-based approach enables early years' educators to plan for a range of lively and imaginative learning situations which will encourage conversation, co-operation and sensory and physical play.

CHRISTMAS ACROSS THE CURRICULUM

Each chapter in this book focuses on a different aspect of Christmas and offers a range of ideas to encourage children's intellectual curiosity, personal and social development, physical play and creative awareness. Chapter 1 (The story of Christmas) enables children to hear, read and re-enact the Nativity story in musical and puppet form. They find out about Bethlehem, make their own stables and think about baby Jesus, and babies everywhere. They also develop an awareness of ordinal number by making a giant Advent calendar.

Chapter 2 (Father Christmas) allows children plenty of scope to 'be' Father Christmas, looking after his reindeer, travelling the world, delivering toys, receiving gifts, having adventures and trying to keep warm. The children learn about the kind St Nicholas, who was the first 'Father Christmas'.

Chapter 3 (Christmas giving) focuses on card making, and the making, giving and sending of Christmas gifts. The children learn, too, about how Christmas was celebrated when their parents and grandparents were children. They learn to think about others, especially on Boxing Day.

Chapter 4 (Festive food) offers ideas to develop children's mathematical and scientific understanding, as they work together to make Christmas 'puddings', fruit punch, edible decorations and 'melting' snowmen. The children's musical, dramatic and language skills are developed in Chapter 5 (Fun and games), which contains ideas for singing, dancing, acting and action games on a festive theme. The children's knowledge and understanding of the world is developed in Chapter 6 (Christmas around the world), in which children learn about Christmas celebrations in various countries and climates.

HOW TO USE THIS BOOK

Themes for early years – Christmas is one of a series of books written specifically for anyone working with young children, whether at home, in playgroups, nursery schools or classes, or reception classes. The book aims to capitalise on children's sense of awe and wonder at Christmas time, based for many, on their own personal experiences of Christmas with their families. The ideas help to develop children's awareness of the communal and universal dimensions of the festival in sensitive and imaginative ways.

The activities are designed to stimulate observation, conversation, and co-operative learning, and can be easily adapted to suit the needs and interests of the children in your care.

TOPIC WEB

To assist you in planning for a broad and balanced curriculum, there is a topic web on pages 8–9. This is fully photocopiable, and is designed to show how each activity relates to the subject areas of the National Curriculum and the Scottish 5–14 Guidelines.

ACTIVITY PAGES

Each chapter in the book focuses on a different aspect of Christmas, and provides a variety of activities to explore the theme. There is one activity on each page, with all activities using the same format for ease of use.

At the beginning of each activity, a learning objective is identified, showing the main curriculum area covered, with a summary of what the children will be doing. This is followed by a suggestion for the optimum number of children in the group, although this will vary according to individual circumstances, such as the ages of your children and the number of adult helpers available and so on. A list of items required is given, followed by a description of any preparation necessary to ensure the success of the activity. The 'What to do' section details easy-to-follow instructions for carrying out the activity, followed by suggestions for stimulating discussion among the children as they engage in the activity. Finally, some follow-up suggestions are given. Always be prepared to be flexible and 'seize the moment' by following up the children's interests, in order to encourage them to become lifelong learners.

DISPLAYS

This section begins with general advice on the importance of creating interactive displays, involving the children at every stage. Such

displays attract 'hands on' participation, encouraging observation and discussion. This is followed by suggestions for creating four specific displays, based on activities in the preceding chapters.

ASSEMBLIES

This chapter provides ideas for planning multicultural assemblies or group sharing times, based on three aspects of Christmas. Each assembly has its own practical ideas on how the children can be encouraged to contribute and reflect on the specific theme. Suggestions for songs and prayers are included.

RESOURCES

This section includes a selection of lively action rhymes, songs, poems and stories all about Christmas, and all of which may be photocopied. Much of this material has been specially commissioned for this book and is directly referred to in many of the activities.

PHOTOCOPIABLE SHEETS

There are eight photocopiable sheets, each linked with a specific activity earlier in the book. Ensure that the children understand how to carry out the activity, and that any new vocabulary is fully explained before they begin. Allow sufficient time to 'talk through' the completed sheet with each child, in order to assess how much they have understood.

RECOMMENDED MATERIALS

Details of story books, information books, song and poetry books and other useful resources are listed on the final page. Always encourage your children to bring in their own 'Christmas' books, too.

EXPRESSIVE ARTS

Planning towards the National Curriculum and the Scottish National guidelines 5–14

MATHEMATICS

ENVIRONMENTAL STUDIES

DESIGN AND TECHNOLOGY

SCIENCE

HISTORY/PEOPLE IN THE PAST

GEOGRAPHY/ PEOPLE AND PLACES

PREPARING FOR PRIMARY SCHOOL

THE NATIONAL CURRICULUM

The National Curriculum was established to standardise the subjects and subject content taught to every child in the country at all levels of education. The intention is that all schools teach the same subjects for the same amount of time each week, so that any child moving to another part of the country is not at a disadvantage. The National Curriculum subjects are: English, Mathematics, Science, History, Geography, Design and Technology, Information Technology, RE, Art, Music and PE.

The National Curriculum programmes of study apply to children who have reached their fifth birthday. Prior to this, an early years' curriculum which is founded on the principles of active learning, first-hand experiences and physical and sensory play, with plenty of time, space and sensitive adult support, will go a long way towards establishing a firm foundation for future learning of the National Curriculum.

THE DESIRABLE OUTCOMES

Before compulsory school, children are working towards Level One of the National Curriculum. The SCAA publication Nursery Education: Desirable Outcomes for Children's Learning on entering compulsory education provides guidance for the education of the under-fives across six Areas of Learning. They are: Personal and Social Development, Language and Literacy, Mathematics, Knowledge and Understanding of the World, Physical Development and Creative Development. The activities in this book, while preparing the children for the National Curriculum, also link closely to these Areas of Learning, following a play-based rationale for learning. Similar guidelines exist for Wales, Scotland and Northern Ireland and the ideas in this book can be applied equally well to the guidance documents published for these countries.

THE SCOTTISH NATIONAL GUIDELINES 5–14

In Scotland, there are National Guidelines for schools on what should be taught to children between the ages of five and fourteen.

These National Guidelines are divided into six main curriculum areas: English Language, Mathematics, Environmental Studies, Expressive Arts, Religious and Moral Education, and Personal and Social Development.

Within these main areas, further subjects are found, for example 'Expressive Arts' includes art and design, drama, music and PE. Strands are also identified within each subject, for example Mathematics includes problem-solving and enquiry, and shape, position and movement.

CHAPTER 1
THE STORY OF CHRISTMAS

From Advent to angels, babies to Bethlehem: in this chapter children read and enact the nativity story and create a giant Advent calendar.

SMILING FACES

Objective

Art – To create a collage of Mary, Joseph, baby Jesus and the Three Wise Men.

Group size

Up to four children.

What you need

Books with pictures of the Three Wise Men visiting Mary, Joseph and baby Jesus, baby and mail order catalogues, scraps of fabric (plain and fancy), silver and coloured foil, lace, ribbon, scissors, glue, a copy for each child of photocopiable page 88 (optional), or pieces of sugar paper and felt-tipped pens.

Preparation

Cut the fabric into small pieces for the children to use to 'clothe' the figures on page 88, or on their own drawings.

What to do

Show the children the pictures in the books of the kind of clothing worn by Mary, Joseph, baby Jesus and the Three Wise men. Either use the figures on page 88 or let the children draw their own on sugar paper. Let the children cut out faces from the catalogues and stick them in the appropriate 'face spaces'. (If the faces are a little too small, the children can add 'hair' with a felt-tipped pen.) Alternatively, the children can use the faces as part of their own drawings. The children can then stick on the fabric pieces to 'clothe' everyone.

Discussion

What sort of clothes would Joseph and Mary have worn, and what colour? What colour were the 'swaddling clothes' of baby Jesus? What do babies usually wear now? What do kings generally wear? What do you think Mary and Joseph would wear today?

Follow-up activities

✧ Let the children cut out a baby's face, a boy's face and a man's face, and draw three pictures – one of Jesus as a baby, one as a boy and one as a man. Use picture bibles for ideas about clothing.

✧ Ask the children to bring in two or three photographs of themselves (as a baby, a toddler, now) and see if other children can put them in order. Bring in three photographs of yourself at different ages (head and shoulders, ideally).

✧ Photocopy the photographs of yourself and let the children cut them out, put them in order, stick them on paper and draw in the rest of you, three times, to show how you have grown!

NATIVITY REBUS

Objective

English – To read a very simple version of the nativity story, with adult support.

Group size

Up to ten.

What you need

Large sheets of white paper, an easel, a bulldog clip, felt-tipped pens, a book depicting the nativity story.

Preparation

Copy the rebus-style version of the nativity story below onto the white paper, sticking a piece of gold paper in the appropriate space at the end. Attach the sheets to an easel with the bulldog clip.

What to do

Tell the story of the nativity to the children. Next, read out your rebus version, pausing before each illustrated word and encouraging the children to supply the word. Place the easel in front of the children and carry out the following steps:

1. Read all the sentences aloud slowly, pointing to each word or picture, one at a time.
2. Repeat step 1, but this time encourage the children to join in with you.
3. Ask the children to read the story aloud together as you point to the words and pictures. Join in occasionally, as necessary, to help the children match their spoken words with the written words.

The nativity story

Mary and Joseph had to go to Bethlehem.

Mary was going to have a .

Mary had to ride on a .

In Bethlehem they could not find anywhere to sleep.

At last they found a .

Baby Jesus was born and Mary put him in a .

Some were looking after their .

They saw a bright light in the sky and some 🕊🕊 .

The 🕊🕊 told them to go and see baby Jesus.

The went to see baby Jesus and gave him a .

The Three Wise Men saw a in the sky and

followed it all the way to the ▦ .

They gave baby Jesus ☆ frankincense and myrrh.

Discussion

Talk about the rebus story, drawing on the children's memories of the full version of the nativity story. Why did Mary and Joseph have to go to Bethlehem? Explain the meaning of any unusual words such as 'manger', 'Frankincense' and so on.

Follow-up activities

✧ Photocopy the rebus story onto A4 sheets and send them home with each child. Copy the three steps from the 'What to do' section above at the top of the first sheet. Substitute the words 'your child' for 'the children'. If possible, practise reading the story individually with each child before he or she takes it home.

✧ Ask the children to bring in nativity story books from home for a display. Write words such as 'Jesus', 'Mary' and 'Joseph' on large cards for the children to 'spot' in their books.

✧ Read the story 'The first Christmas' on page 82, splitting it into sections to read aloud.

WHERE IS BETHLEHEM?

Objective

Geography – To realise that Bethlehem is a real place which can be visited.

Group size

Up to eight children.

What you need

Tables, chairs, a model steering wheel, a pilot's hat, steward's 'uniform', trays, cups, play food, plastic 'walkie-talkie' set (or two replicas made from toothpaste boxes covered in sugar paper), a child's highchair with tray removed (if possible), an atlas, a holiday brochure showing trips to the 'Holy Land'.

Preparation

Set up an 'aeroplane' role play area. Place two chairs, side by side, for the 'pilot' and 'co-pilot', with two chairs facing them. On one, put the model steering wheel for the 'pilot', and on the other, put the atlas, open at the 'world' page, for the 'co-pilot'. Place other chairs for the 'passengers'.

What to do

Let the children enact flying to Bethlehem, with one child as the pilot, one or two as the stewards, one as the 'air traffic controller' who sits in the high chair and the rest as passengers. The 'air traffic controller' must ask the co-pilot at intervals which country the aeroplane is flying over at the moment, en route for Bethlehem. The co-pilot must answer, by referring to the atlas.

Discussion

Tell the children that Bethlehem is in the 'Holy Land', and that many people from all over the world visit Bethlehem, especially at Christmas time. Explain that to visit Bethlehem, people fly either to the countries of Jordan or Israel and point out these places on the atlas. Tell the children that in Bethlehem there is a church called the 'Church of the Nativity', which is built on the spot where many people believe Jesus was born in the stable, and that this church is in Manger Square. Encourage the co-pilot to name the countries of France, Switzerland, Italy and Greece, which aeroplanes often fly over when coming from Great Britain to the 'Holy Land'. Ask if any of the children have visited other countries on holiday.

Follow-up activities

✧ Use a large floor map/atlas and a toy aeroplane – let the children fly the plane above the map, describing the route.
✧ Invite someone who has visited Bethlehem to talk to the children, showing photographs, postcards, slides and so on.
✧ Read the poem 'Busy, busy Bethlehem' on page 67 and ask how the people and animals all got to Bethlehem. How would they get there now?

A LONG WAY

Objective

Music — To recreate the journey of Mary and Joseph through sound effects.

Group size

Ten children, with rest of class watching.

What you need

Pair of coconut shells, plastic jug and bowl, a small table, water, newspaper, a large book, chairs (one for each child), A3 white paper, sugar paper, paints, felt-tipped pens, crayons, coloured chalk, string, pegs, adhesive tape, cassette recorder and blank tape.

Preparation

Line up the chairs in a row. Suspend a long piece of string above and just behind the chairs. Half fill the bowl with water and place this, with the jug, on a small table. Prepare an 'art table' for the children to produce pictures.

What to do

Talk to the children about the sounds they think Mary and Joseph might have heard on their journey from Nazareth to Bethlehem, and discuss ways to create these sounds. Examples are:
• donkey's hooves — coconut shells;

• crackling camp fire — newspaper crumpled and rustled;
• drawing water from a well — bowl of water and jug;
• wind at night — a child's voice;
• wolf howling at night — a child's voice;
• Joseph knocking on doors — child's fist on a large book;
• stable animals (for example a cow, a sheep, a hen and so on) — children's voices;
• Baby Jesus crying — a child's voice.

Let each child choose a sound effect and illustrate that point in the story on an A3 sheet of paper, using paints, crayons and chalks. Peg the pictures in a row on the string to tell a story with the matching 'sound effects' (for example coconut shells) on the chair below each picture.

Allocate each child a chair and tell them they must make the appropriate sound effect. When all the group have had a turn at making sound effects, make a recording of the story. Make the illustrations into a large book, using adhesive tape and sugar paper for a cover. Individual children can read the book while listening to the tape.

Discussion

Talk about how it is seventy miles from Nazareth to Bethlehem, and how this is a very long way to walk. Ask the children whether they think Mary, Joseph and the donkey would be walking quickly or slowly, and why. Ask how they think Mary and Joseph would have managed to have a drink, eat and keep warm during the cold nights, and what dangers they may have experienced on the way. Ask the children about their experiences of long journeys (for example when they might have had to sleep in a car) or of camping trips and so on.

Follow-up activities

✧ Use percussion instruments to make the sounds of an ox, a donkey, a sheep and a cow.
✧ Set up 'journeys' on the floor using road layouts, buildings and play people. Use them to show how, although it is usually quick to travel by car, sometimes it's quicker to walk because of traffic jams, weather conditions, roadwork, traffic accidents and so on.

AWAY IN A MANGER

Objective

Design and Technology – To make individual 3D models of the nativity scene.

Group size

Up to four children.

What you need

A shoe box (without lid) for each child, card, white paper, scissors, felt-tipped pens, paints and brushes, adhesive tape, model farm animals, miniature dolls, toothpaste cartons, pets' bedding or straw, sawdust (from a pet shop) [check that no child is allergic to sawdust or straw], roll of thin bandage or white toilet paper roll, free-standing photograph frames, books showing the nativity scene.

What to do

Show the children the nativity pictures and discuss with them which people and animals they would like to put in their shoe box 'stables'. Ask each child to paint their box. While the 'stables' are drying, support each child in drawing, cutting out and making free-standing card characters and animals, made with a hinged stand at the back. Let the children examine the photograph frames to see how this is done. Younger children may prefer to use this technique just for their human figures but use model farm animals.

Show the children two ways to make a manger and let them choose which to make. Make 'baby Jesus' by drawing and cutting out a tiny card baby or a miniature doll and wrap it in 'swaddling clothes' (strips of narrow bandage

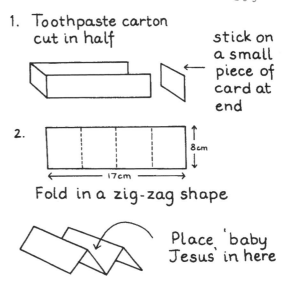

1. Toothpaste carton cut in half

stick on a small piece of card at end

2.

←17cm→

8cm

Fold in a zig-zag shape

Place 'baby Jesus' in here

or white toilet roll paper). Put pets' bedding or straw inside the 'manger'.

When the shoe boxes are dry, turn them on their side, and arrange the figures, animals and 'mangers' inside. Scatter some sawdust or straw on the 'floor'.

Discussion

Ask each child how many people and animals will fit in his/her 'stable'. Will there be room for Mary, Joseph, baby Jesus and the shepherds or the Three Wise Men? Talk about how tall to make the people, so that they look the right size for the 'stable'. Talk about the best way to make the figures stay upright. Ask whether the children would like their figures to stay still ('stationary'), or whether they would like to be able to move them around. Talk about 'swaddling clothes' as well as the meaning of the word 'manger'.

Follow-up activities

✧ Convert the 'stables' into 'nativity puppet theatres'. Cut wide archways on each side of the shoe boxes, and stick a straw to the bottom of each figure instead of the hinged stand so that they may be manoeuvred through the archways.

✧ Create a group nativity scene in a cardboard carton (approximately 45cm × 30cm). Experiment using the figures made for the shoe box 'stables' and let the children realise that they do not look the right size in the carton.

WHAT DID THEY SAY?

Objective

English — To devise dialogue for a nativity puppet play.

Group size

Twelve children, with rest of group watching.

What you need

A washing-line, lightweight curtain(s), twelve chairs, twelve wooden spoons, felt-tipped pens, card, scissors, small pieces of fabric, ribbon, adhesive tape.

Preparation

Line up the chairs in a row. Suspend the washing-line in front of the chairs and fold the curtain(s) over the line. Ensure the line is high enough to hide the children from view when they are sitting on the chairs, holding up their wooden spoon puppets.

What to do

Make some character puppets with the children (to include Mary, Joseph, the innkeeper, four shepherds and three Wise Men) by drawing faces on the top of the spoons using a felt-tipped pen, and then adding fabric and ribbon to decorate. One child could make a 'donkey' puppet by cutting out some card in the shape of a donkey, colouring it and then sticking it to the top of the spoon with adhesive tape. Another child could make a 'Jesus in the manger' puppet in a similar way.

Ask the children to each sit on a chair, ready to hold up their puppet. You tell the story, and at each point pause for the child to add dialogue. For example 'Joseph heard that the Emperor wanted everyone to go back to where they were born to be counted. Joseph was very worried about this and he said to Mary...'. 'When Mary heard this news, she was very worried, too, and she said...'. Practise a few times with the initial twelve children before performing in front of the rest of the group.

Discussion

Encourage the children to think about what the characters might have said by talking about how they might have been feeling (happy, sad, worried, afraid) and why. Talk about expression and encourage the children to try talking in a 'happy voice' or a 'sad voice' and so on. Discuss how babies communicate and talk about the difference between crying and gurgling.

Follow-up activities

✧ Play 'Who said that?' in which you think of a sentence and the children have to guess who might have said it. Some of the children might like to be the 'teacher'.

✧ Read the poem 'Look at the baby' on page 67 to illustrate one idea about what the animals say.

✧ Use the display idea on page 60 to make a group nativity scene.

GIANT ADVENT CALENDAR

Objective

Mathematics — To learn about ordinal numbers.

Group size

Up to four.

What you need

A large piece of card (84cm × 60cm), smaller pieces of coloured card, white paper, a large calendar, a commercially produced Advent calendar, scissors, felt-tipped pens, pencil, adhesive tape, old Christmas cards, glue, glitter, ribbon, Blu-Tack.

Preparation

In pencil, draw 24 rectangles (each 8cm × 6cm) spaced at intervals on the large card. In the top right-hand corner of each rectangle write 1st, 2nd, 3rd and so on up to 24th. Cut the pieces of coloured card and white paper into 24 rectangles (also 8cm × 6cm).

What to do

Ask each child to think of an activity which we do before Christmas, and to draw this on a rectangular piece of white paper. Some children may prefer to cut out an appropriate object, or scene from an old Christmas card, and to stick this on the white paper. Discuss with each child whether this activity could be carried out 'a long time before Christmas' or 'just before Christmas' (for example on Christmas Eve).

Decide together on which rectangle of the large card to stick each activity picture. When each child has done this, give them a coloured rectangle on which to over-write, copy or draw a large number to correspond with their chosen 'day' on the large card. Help each child to write 'st', 'nd', 'rd' or 'th' as appropriate, in the top right-hand corner of each square. Each child can then stick a little glitter onto their card. Finally, help each child to stick their coloured card on top of their activity picture, using adhesive tape down the left-hand side of the card, to make a little 'door'. Secure each 'door' with a little Blu-Tack. Write 'Our Advent calendar' at the top of the large card and decorate it with ribbons.

Discussion

Explain that one of the meanings of the word 'Advent' is the coming of Christmas Day, and the days from December 1st until Christmas Day. Show the children a large wall calendar and recite with them '1st, 2nd, 3rd and so on as you point to each square. Do the same with the commercially produced Advent calendar. Tell the children that in the 24 days leading up to Christmas Eve, lots of things can be prepared for Christmas Day. Ask the children for their ideas, for example cooking, shopping, making cards and presents and so on.

Follow-up activities

✧ Make the Advent calendar in November and present it to another class, hospital, old people's home and so on in time for December 1st.
✧ Talk about the twelve days of Christmas and sing the carol, changing the words to 'On the first day of Christmas this is what I played with — one jigsaw' and so on.

PRESENTS FOR JESUS

Objective

RE – To think about being kind to babies.

Group size

Up to six children.

What you need

A soft toy lamb, pictures of gold, frankincense and myrrh, items to buy and sell in a 'baby shop' (for example baby clothes, doll's cot, buggy, pram, bath, highchair), baby toys and books, baby food and so on, large peel-off labels, felt-tipped pen, play coins and notes, scissors, 'cheque books' (made from stapled paper strips), old plastic 'cash card', cash till, telephone, writing pad, pencil, wallets, purses, shopping bags, dolls in assorted sizes, tables, chairs.

Preparation

Set up a 'baby shop' with the children. Include a 'babies" play area with chairs around it where 'customers' who are waiting to be served may sit. Depending on the ages and experience of the children, price everything in pennies or use amounts the children can understand.

What to do

Hold up the soft toy lamb and the pictures of gold, frankincense and myrrh, and ask the children who gave these presents to baby Jesus. Then let the children enact going to a 'baby shop' to buy a present for a baby. Let the children take their babies to play in the 'play area'.

If appropriate, let the children use 'cheque books' and 'cash cards'. Encourage the 'cashiers' to use the telephone to order large items and to write down delivery details on the writing pad.

Discussion

Talk about the gifts from the shepherds and the Three Wise Men. Explain that now, instead of giving a baby real gold, some people like to give money to a baby, but that this is usually kept at the bank until the baby is older. Talk about the sweet-smelling frankincense and myrrh that would help Mary and Joseph when they prayed to God to say 'thank you' for baby Jesus. Ask what special presents the children would make or buy for a baby, and what people gave them when they were babies.

Follow-up activities

✧ Ask the children and parents to bring in any presents they received as babies (perhaps for a Christening) and make a display.
✧ Make a collection of outgrown baby toys and clothes to send to a charity in this country or abroad.
✧ Photocopy the star designs on page 89 onto card to make a mobile as a present for a baby. Cut out the stars and decorate them with crayon and glitter. Secure two straws in an 'x' shape with adhesive tape. Hang the stars on the straws with invisible thread, and hang the mobile from the ceiling with a loop of invisible thread.

CHAPTER 2
FATHER CHRISTMAS

The importance of Father Christmas for young children is paramount at Christmas, and the ideas in this chapter provide the chance to learn about St Nicholas, and make presents and clothes for Father Christmas. The children can also pretend to be Father Christmas, looking after his reindeer and delivering presents around the world.

A PRESENT FOR SANTA

Objective

Design and Technology – To make a gift for Santa.

Group size

Four children.

What you need

Catalogues, small food cartons and so on, masking tape, adhesive tape, glue, milk bottle tops, lids, paints, scissors, felt-tipped pens, card, a hole punch, Christmas wrapping paper, decorative twine, a large work table, newspaper, a smaller table.

Preparation

Spread out the reclaimed modelling materials on the smaller table. Cut the card into 'luggage label' shapes and punch a hole in each one. Cover the work table with newspaper.

What to do

Let the children browse through the gift catalogues to get some ideas for what Santa might like as a present. Once they have decided what to make, support each child as necessary to carry out their designs. Show them how to use masking tape to secure cartons together, and glue to stick on lids to represent 'buttons' and so on. When each child has made a gift, ask them to estimate the amount of wrapping paper needed to wrap the present. Let the children wrap the gifts and give them a label each on which to overwrite, copy or write, 'To Santa, Love from ...'. Tie the labels to the gifts with twine, and let the children take them home to put out for Santa on Christmas Eve.

Discussion

Talk about how Santa is a 'grown-up'. Ask the children what sort of presents 'grown-ups' might like to receive. Ask them what they think Santa would like, and why, for example a letter rack (for all the children's letters); a personal portable stereo (to listen to on the journey); a picnic basket (to put his food in so he won't be hungry on the journey) and so on.

Follow-up activities

✧ Ask the children to think of presents that Rudolph and the reindeer might like (for example hot water bottles, blankets, 'reindeer' food and so on).
✧ Let the children think of presents that some 'grown-ups' in their family might like and complete the photocopiable sheet on page 90. They have to draw faces of relatives in the ovals, writing their names underneath and drawing a gift for each one in the 'gift boxes'.
✧ Tell the children that Santa has a workshop where he makes toys for children, and sing the song 'Father Christmas makes the toys' on page 75.

REINDEER'S BEDTIME

Objective

English – To read the names of Santa's reindeer by recognising letters and initial sounds.

Group size

Four children.

What you need

Nine model reindeer (use farm horses or cut out models), tiny piece of red crêpe paper, adhesive tape, scissors, card, felt-tipped pen, nine miniature breakfast cereal packets, small amount of straw (from a pet shop), a 'Santa' hat, pipe-cleaners, white material (enough to cover children's table), an awl.

Preparation

Dasher | Vixen | Blitzen | Dancer | Comet | Prancer | Donner | Cupid | Rudolph

↑
straw

Cut off the fronts of the packets and stick them all together in a row, with adhesive tape, making a line of 'reindeer shelters'. Cut out eighteen small cards and write the names of each reindeer twice. Stick a name card above each 'shelter'. Stick the crêpe paper on the nose of one reindeer to represent 'Rudolph'. Make a hole with an awl through the remaining name cards and thread a pipe-cleaner through each one. Secure each card to a reindeer. Cover the table with the white material to represent 'snow'. Place the 'shelters' down one side of the table.

What to do

Tell the children that every year, after delivering all the presents to children everywhere, Santa makes sure that each reindeer has a good sleep in its own 'shelter'. Say that Santa always kindly scatters some straw on the floor of each 'shelter' to make sure the reindeer are comfortable.

Let each child take turns to be 'Santa', passing around the hat. With each child, give him or her a reindeer, saying its name, and see if 'Santa' can put it in its correct 'shelter', scattering a little straw on the 'floor' first. Help the children match the names by emphasising initial letter sounds and also the 'look' of the whole word.

Discussion

Talk about how places and objects are often named, so that people know where to keep their belongings, and do not get them mixed up with other people's. Ask the children to think of examples (such as names on coat pegs, name labels in clothes and so on). Ask the children if any have a name plaque on their bedroom door or any other 'named' items (for example mugs, hairbands and so on).

Follow-up activities

✧ Take all the name tags from the reindeer. Ask the children to find the correct shelters for each one, after telling them the correct name, helping with clues if necessary. Help those children who are ready, to discriminate between the names 'Dancer' and 'Donner' by 'sounding out' the first three letters.

✧ Stick cards of first names to two or three 'reindeer' children with adhesive tape. See if a 'Santa' can lead them to their name-labelled 'shelters' underneath tables.

SAINT NICHOLAS

Objective

History – To learn about the story of Saint Nicholas, the first 'Father Christmas'.

Group size

Whole group then small groups of five children.

What you need

A play barrel, two tables, a piece of string, adhesive tape, three pairs of adult-sized bed socks, card, scissors, six pegs, six £1 coins, a fancy cloak, a 'patched' blanket, three long skirts, playbricks.

Preparation

Arrange two tables side by side, with a space between to allow the play barrel to be placed above the space, safely supported by the tables. Suspend a piece of string across the space by securing each end on a table with adhesive tape. Place the barrel (the 'chimney') to represent a fireplace, and build a playbrick 'hearth'. Cut the card into six pieces and curl each one to make a cylinder shape which will fit inside each sock to make it semi-rigid.

What to do

Tell the story of 'St Nicholas' on page 81. Then let the whole group mime some key points of the story and think about what the people might have said or been thinking about. Such key points could be:

• The poor family looking sad as they opened cupboards in their home to find no food.
• The poor man looking sad as he walked along and Nicholas asking him what was wrong. The daughters washing, squeezing and hanging up their stockings.
• Nicholas climbing on to the roof and dropping the coins down the chimney.

• The family looking delighted as they find the money.

When the whole group have mimed, choose five children at a time to mime or act out the whole story in front of everyone else. (Hold the hand of the child playing St Nicholas, as they climb on and off the table, for safety.)

Discussion

Talk about how when Nicholas and Jesus grew up they were very kind to poor and sick people and gave them charity. Ask the children what they think this word means and whether they or their families have ever given money to charity. Explain that Nicholas would not have worn a red suit, because people did not think of that idea until a long time after he had died.

Follow-up activities

✧ Adopt a special Christmas charity and make a 'Charity box' (see also 'Boxes for Boxing Day' on page 34). Bring some charity Christmas cards in to show the children and talk about them, mentioning any charity shops in your area.

✧ Ask if the children have heard stories about other saints such as St Christopher and St George. Mention Mother Theresa of Calcutta, and how people think that she might become a saint because of all her kindness to poor and sick people.

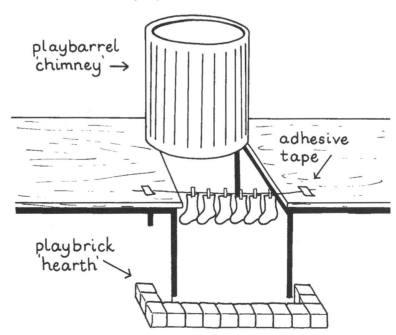

playbarrel 'chimney' →

adhesive tape

playbrick 'hearth'

WHICH WAY, RUDOLPH?

Objective

Geography — To learn the names of four regions of the world.

Group size

Two at a time, with larger group watching.

What you need

Globe and/or map of the world, Santa's hat, sledge, sleigh bells, brown paper, scissors, adhesive tape, red nose (or face paints/red chalk), card, felt-tipped pens, model polar bear, penguin, panda, buffalo, floor space.

Preparation

Make a pair of 'antlers' from brown paper. Cut the card into four rectangles (each 15cm x 10cm). Draw a large fish on the first piece, a small fish on the second, some green bamboo shoots on the third and some grass on the fourth. Fold four more pieces of card (each 21cm x 15cm) horizontally, so they stand up, and label each 'North Pole', 'South Pole', 'China' and 'America' respectively.

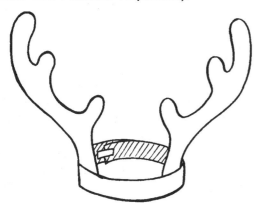

What to do

Place the labels around the floor. Put the polar bear next to the 'North Pole' label, the penguin by the 'South Pole' label, the panda next to the 'China' label, and the buffalo next to the 'America' label. Point out these places on the globe and/or map, mentioning the animals who live there and what they like to eat. Hold up the cards of the animals' 'food'.

Let one child be Father Christmas and sit in the sledge with the sleigh bells and 'food' cards. Let another child be Rudolph, wearing a red nose and 'antlers'. Explain that one night before Christmas, Father Christmas and Rudolph decided to take some special food to four animals around the world. Explain that Rudolph must pull Father Christmas around the world, delivering the big fish to the polar bear, the little fish to the penguin, the bamboo to the panda, and the sweet, juicy grass to the buffalo.

Discussion

Do you know where Father Christmas lives? Is it hot or cold there? Which animal would be nearest to Father Christmas? Mention the terms 'Arctic' (North Pole) and 'Antarctic' (South Pole), and say that it is cold in the South Pole too. Do the children know the names of any other polar animals? Would they like to live at the North or South Pole? What would it be like? Talk about how there are not many pandas left in the world.

Follow-up activities

✧ Ask the children to draw simple maps to show Santa's travels around the world.
✧ Sing 'Jingle bells' adding the names of different places for example, 'Oh, what fun it is to ride to London on a sleigh!'.

OVER THE ROOF TOPS

Objective

PE — To practise balancing skills in a fantasy Christmas context.

Group size

Four children, with rest of group watching and joining in singing.

What you need

A play barrel, balancing beam(s), climbing cube/steps, stool and so on (to represent 'roof tops'), cotton wool, adhesive tape, a 'Santa hat', pillow case (for 'sack'), two food cartons, Christmas wrapping paper, child's sledge, a set of sleigh bells, red nose (or face paints/red chalk), three sets of 'antlers' (if possible) — see 'Which way, Rudolph?' on page 22, a copy of the song 'Santa, Santa' on page 74.

Preparation

Arrange the beam(s) and so on around the floor space. Make sure the children are comfortably dressed or changed into loose clothing and wearing plimsolls or bare feet. Wrap the food cartons in Christmas paper to represent 'presents'. Place them inside the 'sack' in the sledge, in the middle of the floor space. Decorate the top of the play barrel with cotton wool 'snow', secured with adhesive tape. Practise the song 'Santa, Santa' a few times with the children.

What to do

Choose a child to be 'Santa' to wear the hat, carry the bells and sit in the sledge with the 'sack'. Choose another to be 'Rudolph' and wear the red nose. The other two children are 'helper reindeer' who wear 'antlers', but do not have red noses.

The three 'reindeer' pull 'Santa' around the floor space while all four children and the rest of the watching group sing the song 'Santa, Santa'. At the end of the song, 'Santa' gets out of the sleigh with the sack, and balancing carefully, walks across the 'roof tops' to the 'chimney'. 'Santa' climbs inside, takes the 'presents' out of the 'sack', emerges from the chimney and walks back to the sledge. Let all the children have a turn to be Santa. The 'reindeer' conclude the activity by pulling Santa around again, as everyone sings the song one more time.

Provide support for 'Santa' as he walks across the beams and climbs in and out of the 'chimney'. If you do not have beams available put down floor mats to walk along.

Discussion

Should Santa walk quickly or slowly over the roof tops? Why? What would Santa wear on his feet? Why? Ask the children about their winter footwear. What would it be like to be 'Santa's helper' and ride with him in his sleigh? Ask the children whether they know what chimneys are, and whether any children have open fires and/or fireplaces in their homes.

Follow-up activities

✧ Dress a doll as Santa and make a miniature presents 'sack'. Put Santa in a 'sleigh' made from a carton and let one child, 'Rudolph', pull the 'sleigh' along the 'roof tops', and lift out 'Santa' to deliver the presents down the 'chimney'.
✧ Make prints of the soles of the children's (wellington) boots.

A CHRISTMAS COLLAR

Objective

English – To make up stories about some of Father Christmas's exciting 'deliveries'.

Group size

Five children.

What you need

A small, soft toy dog, a sheet of writing paper, a stamped envelope, felt-tipped pens, section of an old belt, Christmas wrapping paper, A3 sheets of drawing paper, pillow case with a hole in the bottom.

Preparation

Write a 'letter', supposedly from a small boy, asking Father Christmas for a new collar for his pet dog. Address the envelope to 'Father Christmas, North Pole'. Make a miniature 'dog

collar' to fit the toy dog from a piece of belt. Draw a picture of 'Rudolph' wearing a 'reindeer collar' around his neck.

What to do

Put the dog, the letter in its envelope, the 'dog collar', the wrapping paper, the pillow case with the hole, and the picture of 'Rudolph' on the table. Let the children sit around the table and talk about the items, and see if they can collectively make up a story about them, perhaps similar to this 'plot':

A small boy writes to Father Christmas, asking for a new collar for his pet dog. Father Christmas wraps up the gift and puts it in his sack, but sadly it drops out, through a hole, into the night sky, as Father Christmas is riding along in his sleigh. Father Christmas is very sad about it, but luckily notices that Rudolph is wearing a 'reindeer collar'. Rudolph kindly agrees to give his collar to the little boy for his dog. Father Christmas wraps it up in some spare paper he always carries, delivers the present, making the little boy and his dog very happy.

Encourage all the children to contribute some ideas to the group story.

Discussion

What did the little boy ask Father Christmas for? What do you think had happened to the dog's old collar? Did Father Christmas say yes? What sad thing happened on the journey? Who was very kind? Have you ever given somebody something of yours?

Follow-up activities

✧ Let the children cut out the pictures on photocopiable page 90. They should jumble them up and try to arrange them in the correct order.
✧ Let the children find two or three objects in the nursery/classroom to give to you to include in a Father Christmas story. Then you may give the children some objects (for example soft toy animals) for them to use in made-up Christmas stories.
✧ Teach the children 'Santa Claus action rhyme' on page 68. Let them devise their own finger actions to represent their 'Santa' adventures, and also the events in the 'Rudolph's collar' story.

KEEP WARM SANTA!

Objective

Science — To experiment with coverings to keep a model 'Santa' warm.

Group size

Four children.

What you need

Two plastic babies' feeding bottles, a kettle, water, table, red card, adhesive tape, beige card, scissors, felt-tipped pens, cotton wool, glue, six small black buttons, a red cotton shirt, a small piece of red cotton material, a child's anorak, a piece of quilted material (preferably red), a clock.

Preparation

Cut out rectangle shapes from the red card (each 10cm × 2cm), and stick them on either side of the bottles to make 'arms' for the two model 'Santas'. Cut out two oval shapes from the beige card for the models' 'faces'. Cut out two miniature 'tabard' shapes to fit the bottle (one from the red cotton, and one from the quilted material). Fill the kettle with water and place it on a table, preferably adjacent to an electric socket, so that a hot kettle does not have to be carried near the children.

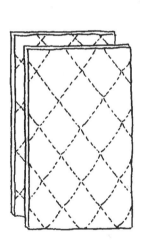

What to do

Let two children draw faces on the ovals for the two model 'Santas', sticking on cotton wool for hair and beards. The third and fourth children may stick the buttons on the 'tabards'. Help the children to stick the faces on the bottles with adhesive tape, and to put on the 'tabards', closing the sides with adhesive tape.

Hold up the red cotton shirt and ask if this would keep Santa warm. Ask the same question as you hold up an anorak. Very carefully, unpick some stitches in the bottom corner of

the anorak to reveal the warm, quilted lining. Say that the two model 'Santas' will help us find out which material would keep Santa the warmer. Boil the kettle and carefully fill the bottles well away from the children, but in their sight. Tell the children that 'Santa' is having a hot drink to 'warm him up'.

Encourage the children to predict which 'Santa' will stay the warmest after five minutes, based on their own experiences of wearing warm clothes in cold weather. Leave the model 'Santas' in their 'coats' for five minutes, then carefully remove them. Let the children carefully touch the 'Santas' (under adult supervision) to see which one has stayed the warmest.

Discussion

Say that our bodies must stay warm all the time. How does your hand feel if you put it

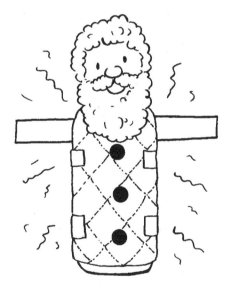

down the back of your collar and leave it there for a few minutes? What is inside our bodies that makes us warm? How can we keep warm, especially in cold weather? What sort of clothes should we wear to keep warm? Which coat was warmer?

Follow-up activities

✧ Read 'A busy time for Mrs Christmas' on page 83, about when Santa had a cold.
✧ Let the children sort clothes into 'Warm for winter' and 'Cool for summer'.

SANTA'S CLOTHES

Objective

Mathematics – To match the dots on a giant dice with the corresponding numerals.

Group size

Up to six children.

What you need

Large sheets of kitchen paper, card, adhesive tape, scissors, black felt-tipped pen, glue, cotton wool, a child's vest, pants, a 'Santa' hat, a child's shirt, jumper, red anorak or jacket, belt, red trousers, a pair of gloves, socks and wellingtons, one scarf, one chair for each child, a giant foam dice.

Preparation

Cut the card into 15 rectangles, each the size of a small envelope. Make two sets of cards numbered 1 to 6 (to make 12 cards). Write the numerals 3, 4 and 5 on the remaining three cards. Stick a card on each item of clothing (use adhesive tape): vest = 1; shirt = 2; jumper = 3; anorak = 4; hat = 5; belt = 6; pants = 1; trousers = 2; socks = 3 each; wellingtons = 4 each; gloves = 5 each; scarf = 6.

Stick the kitchen paper sheets together with adhesive tape so they are large enough for a child to lie down on. Ask a child to lie on the paper and draw around him/her. Tell the children that the outline is going to be 'Santa'. Let the children draw a face and stick on the cotton wool for a beard. Arrange Santa's numbered clothes in a row, next to the outline. Let each child sit on a chair, side by side.

What to do

Tell the children they are going to help Santa to get dressed. Each child throws the dice, counts the spots and selects a corresponding item of clothing. He or she must then put the item in the correct position on the outline. The children must think about a sensible order for placing the clothes in position (for example the vest cannot be put on top of the anorak!).

If a child throws a number which corresponds to an item of clothing which cannot logically be put in position at that point, the child must miss a turn. Similarly, if a number has already been used, they miss a turn.

Discussion

Talk about how important it is to put clothes on in the correct order, and on the correct part of the body. Have the children any amusing stories about how when they were very little they 'got it wrong'?

Follow-up activities

✧ For fun, let the children dress a large teddy the wrong way!

✧ Photocopy the sheet on page 92 and give one to each child. Pair the children and let them share a dice. Explain that they should colour in the corresponding part on the 'Santa' according to the throw, and miss a turn if they have already thrown the number. The winner is the first to complete their 'Santa'.

CHAPTER 3
A TIME FOR GIVING

The pleasure of giving at Christmas is explored as children make and send cards and presents. The activities encourage children to think about other people who may be less fortunate than themselves.

HOW HEAVY AND HOW MUCH?

Objective

Mathematics – To weigh 'Christmas parcels'.

Group size

Five children.

What you need

'Heavy' and 'light' objects for demonstration purposes (for example a straw hat and a lightweight plastic wastepaper bin), baking scales (up to 5kg), lightweight tray, selection of objects weighing approximately 1kg, 2kg, 3kg, 4kg and 5kg, sugar paper, scissors, adhesive tape, extra large plastic carrier bag, large and small peel-off labels, coins, a table as a 'Post Office' counter.

Preparation

Give the children plenty of experience of 'weighing' objects in their hands, to say whether they feel heavy or light and to compare them (heavier than/lighter than). Ensure that they handle large, light objects as well as small, heavy objects. Write amounts (for example 25p, 50p, £1) on the small labels for 'stamps'.

What to do

Help four children in the group to choose a gift each and help them to wrap their gifts with sugar paper. Ask each child who their gift is for, and help them write the name and address on a large peel-off label (so that the sugar paper wrapping may be reused). Let them write their own names and address on a 'sender's' label.

The children take their 'parcels' to the 'Post Office person', who weighs the parcels, tells them how much it will cost to send and stick 'stamps' on the parcels. The 'customers' then pay their money. (When the 'pan' on the scales is too small for the size of the 'parcels', replace it with a lightweight tray, remembering to adjust the scales 'needle' to zero).

Discussion

Talk about how it costs money to send parcels, depending on the weight of the parcel and its destination. Would paper or a plastic bag be better for wrapping up, say, balls? Why? (Tell the children never to play with plastic bags.) Talk about 'kilograms' and 'grams', and weighing cookery ingredients. Talk about what happens to parcels when they leave the Post Office. Have you ever received a parcel in the post? How did you feel?

Follow-up activities

✧ Take a small group to a local Post Office to send a small package, for example a gift to a sick child.
✧ Ask the children to bring in used British and overseas stamps to stick on a poster headed 'Stamps from around the world'.

POT POURRI BASKETS

Objective

Design and Technology – To make a pot pourri basket as a Christmas gift.

Group size

Four children.

What you need

One mini cereal box per child, scissors, adhesive tape, coloured card, metallic paper, glue, peel-off adhesive shapes, felt-tipped pens, aluminium foil, pot pourri, a hole punch, decorative twine.

Preparation

Cut along one long edge of each box to remove the 'lid', open out the box and flatten it. Cut the metallic paper into small squares. Cut the coloured card into strips (each 25cm × 2cm) to make handles for the baskets. Cut the card into small, rectangular 'gift tags', each with decorative twine threaded through a hole.

What to do

Let the children work in pairs to reassemble their boxes 'inside out', so that they are now

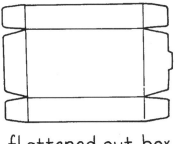

flattened out box

'white boxes'. Help each pair to secure the corners with adhesive tape.

Ask the children to decorate the sides of their 'baskets' by gluing on metallic squares, using adhesive shapes or drawing with felt-tipped pens. Help the children to line their baskets with aluminium foil and then to fill them with pot pourri. Add a coloured card strip 'handle', secured with adhesive tape. Help the children to write their 'gift tags' and to tie them to the basket handles.

Discussion

Who do you think would like to receive your basket for Christmas? Where would be a good place for them to keep it? Do you know what pot pourri is, and how it is made? Can you think of anything else people use to make their homes smell nice (for example flowers, scented candles, aromatherapy vaporisers and so on).

Follow-up activities

✧ Give the children magnifying glasses to examine the petals, flower heads and so on in the pot pourri. Provide card or paper, glue, crayons or felt-tipped pens and let the children make flowery collages using the pot pourri.

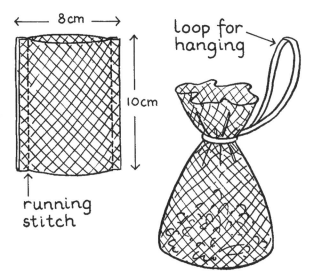

✧ Make pot pourri sachets for drawers, or to hang on clothes hangers in wardrobes. Cut cellular paper kitchen cloth into rectangles (10cm × 8cm). Let the children secure the two edges with running stitches, put some pot pourri inside and tie up the top with ribbon or decorative twine.

WHAT CAN IT BE?

Objective

Mathematics — To recognise the properties of 3D shapes.

Group size

Up to ten children.

What you need

A chair, a 'screen' (for example a puppet theatre, or curtain on a rope), Christmas wrapping paper, scissors, adhesive tape, everyday items which are cubes, cuboids, spheres and cylinders (two or three of each — such as a dice, a building block, a stock cube, a ball, an orange, a grapefruit, a rolling pin [without handles], a hair roller, a telescope), an easel, large piece of paper, felt-tipped pen.

Preparation

Wrap each item up tightly in Christmas paper. Make a chart of 3D shapes, and stick on the easel. Place the chair behind the 'screen'.

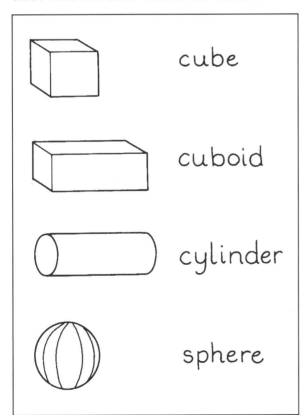

What to do

Ask the children to look around the room, to 'spot' the solid shapes on the chart. Hold up two, different wrapped items and see if the children can name the shapes, and say how they are the same and different.

Sit one child on the chair behind the screen and give him or her one item to hold, without the 'audience' seeing which one. The 'audience' must guess whether it is a cube, cuboid, cylinder or a sphere by asking various questions. Encourage the children to look at the chart to help them think of a question. Once the children have guessed what kind of shape it is, the child may emerge from behind the screen and sit with the parcel on view. All the children must now try and guess what is underneath the wrapping paper.

Discussion

As the children look at the chart, encourage them to ask questions such as: Does it have straight edges? Does it have corners? Does it have sides? Is it curved? Can it roll? Is it round all over? Ask if they can think of presents they have received which are cubes/cylinders and so on.

Follow-up activities

✧ Make a 'feely box' from an upturned fruit carton, with two holes cut in the side. Inside put tightly wrapped items with interesting shapes (for example a cricket bat, tennis racquet, coat hanger, sieve and so on).
✧ Let the children practise their folding skills by wrapping up building bricks in tissue or crêpe paper, and securing them with adhesive tape. Use them in an attractive 3D display (for example under a Christmas tree, or peeping out of Santa's bag).
✧ Teach the children the rhyme 'What's in the parcel?' on page 69 and play 'Pass the parcel' together.

I WISH YOU A MERRY CHRISTMAS!

Objective

Art – To make a creative Christmas card using a variety of media.

Group size

Six children.

What you need

Individual passport-sized photographs of the children's faces, card, scissors, glue, collage materials, paints, felt-tipped pens, a selection of old Christmas cards, photocopier.

Preparation

Send a letter to parents, asking them to send in passport-sized photographs (or larger ones to trim) of their children's faces, or, alternatively, photocopies of photographs. Ask permission to trim the photographs for the purpose of making the cards. Trim the photographs so that only the faces and hair are visible. Cut the card and fold into Christmas card sizes.

What to do

Let the children browse through the Christmas cards and ask them to choose one simple Christmas 'character', 'place' or 'object' to cut out such as Father Christmas, his sleigh, a snowman, a Christmas tree and so on. Help the children, as necessary, to cut these out and to stick them on the front of their own cards.

Next, they can stick their own faces on top of any faces on the cut-outs, if appropriate, or in a suitable place (for example next to a Christmas tree), and add their 'body' by drawing or with collage materials. Let them add further details to complete the 'picture', by drawing, or sticking on collage items (for example silver stars, cotton wool snow flakes, squares of Christmas paper to represent presents and so on). The children can then overwrite, copy or write a message inside the card.

Discussion

Ask the children to imagine themselves in the situation depicted in their own pictures. Ask what they would be thinking, feeling or saying or what they might be doing later, for example Father Christmas might have delivered all his presents and be about to go home for a hot meal!

Follow-up activities

✧ Make speech bubbles for the picture of themselves on their cards.
✧ Sing the song 'Christmas giving' on page 76 together.
✧ Draw around the shape of one child on card and let the children turn the outline into Father Christmas by using red paint, cotton wool and so on. Cut out an oval space for his face and hang up the figure on a piece of suspended string with pegs. Let the children take turns to be 'Father Christmas', by standing behind the card, with their faces showing through the 'face hole'.

WILL IT FIT?

Objective

Mathematics – To develop awareness of shape and space.

Group size

Six to eight children.

What you need

A selection of different sized Christmas cards and their envelopes, different sized Christmas parcels, including those with awkward shapes, 'Christmas stockings' (for example large, baggy, adult-sized bed socks), pillowcases, an egg timer.

Preparation

Scatter the Christmas cards and envelopes on the floor inside 'Father Christmas's house' (possibly the home corner). Position the parcels near the pillowcases and the Christmas stockings.

What to do

Pretend that Father Christmas is in a muddle because he must send all his Christmas cards before rushing off to deliver all the Christmas parcels. Unfortunately, he has dropped his box of Christmas cards on the floor and they need matching with the correct envelopes. Use an egg timer to see if pairs of children can match cards with envelopes before the timer runs out.

To provide more practice with shapes, ask the children to help Father Christmas by testing out the best way to pack a 'Christmas stocking' and a pillowcase with the maximum number of toys.

Discussion

How can you check whether a card matches an envelope? Which is better – holding card and envelope in separate hands or placing the card on top of the envelope? Which shaped parcels fit together? Is it easier to pack a pillowcase or a 'Christmas stocking?' Do the children find they can fit more presents in the stocking if the tiny items are positioned in the 'toe'?

Follow-up activities

✧ Let the children make their own cards with envelopes to match. Measure their cards against a commercially-produced envelope and find one that will be large enough. Show them how to open out the envelope carefully, lay it flat and then draw around the envelope 'template' on paper, fold it and use a small amount of glue to secure the edges.

✧ Recite the poem 'Our Christmas cards' on page 69 with the children.

✧ Let the children try packing a suitcase for a winter holiday and seeing if all the bulky jackets, jumpers and boots and so on will fit inside.

WHAT DID YOU GET?

Objective

English – To develop memory, listening and speaking skills.

Group size

Six to eight children.

What you need

A small replica Christmas parcel (for example small box wrapped in Christmas paper and ribbons), one chair for each child.

Preparation

Make the replica gift and arrange the chairs in a circle.

Discussion

Tell the children that it will help their memory if they try 'to see a picture inside their heads' of each child in front of them in the game, playing with their named toy. If a child does have difficulty in remembering what has been said previously, give the child a clue, such as, 'It's an animal beginning with the sound of 't'.' Alternatively, ask the children to make up clues.

Follow-up activities

✧ Let the children draw pictures of their toys, writing their own names on the back of the paper. See if other children can match the pictures with their 'artists'.

✧ Can the children remember who gave them each of their presents, in order to write a short 'Thank you' note to each person? (Provide assistance as required.)

What to do

Play this game just after the Christmas holiday, when the children's memories of the festivities are fresh. Give one child the 'parcel' to hold and ask him or her to name one present he or she received for Christmas. The child then passes the 'parcel' to the next child in the circle, who then says, for example 'Thomas got a train set and I got a doll's house'. This child then passes the 'parcel' to the next child who says, 'Thomas got a train set, Poojah got a doll's house, and I got a jigsaw'. The children then carry on around the circle, trying to remember what everyone has said before them.

✧ Can the children remember any of the presents that different members of their family received for Christmas?

✧ Send a letter to parents saying that on a certain day you will be holding 'Christmas Sharing Day', when each child may bring in one present he or she received (preferably without too many small parts). Encourage the children to share their toys with one another, explaining how they work, the rules of any game, what happens in a story and so on.

✧ Make a Christmas presents display using the idea on page 61.

WHEN GRANNY WAS LITTLE

Objective

History — To learn how Christmas celebrations have changed over time.

Group size

Whole class.

What you need

Paper, felt-tipped pens, photocopied letter (see 'Preparation' below), a large empty class book made out of sheets of thick sugar paper.

Preparation

Send a letter home to parents and grandparents asking them to jot down one memory of Christmas from their childhoods, particularly those incidents that would not be likely to occur nowadays. Be sensitive to individual family circumstances. For those children whose families do not celebrate Christmas, adapt the letter to focus on another appropriate festival or celebration.

What to do

Ask the children to use felt-tipped pens to draw a picture of the memories sent in by their parents and grandparents and help them to overwrite, copy or draw a simple caption.

Stick the pictures in a class book, starting with all the memories sent in by the parents and then those sent in by grandparents. After displaying the finished books, include them in the class library.

Discussion

How did Christmas celebrated by parents and grandparents differ from celebrations today in terms of food, presents, worship, television and family traditions? Did people sing the same carols and songs? Did families gather together in larger groups? Did grandparents sit down to watch the Queen's speech on television? What games that were popular fifty years ago are still played today at Christmas? What do the children think they would have enjoyed about Christmas in the past? What wouldn't they have liked?

Follow up activities

✧ Make a collection of popular toys given as presents to the children's grandparents, for example Dinky cars, marbles, Hornby train sets, china dolls.
✧ Ask a grandparent or a great-grandparent to come in to talk to the children about their Christmas celebrations.
✧ Invite grandparents to send in old photographs of family Christmases and set up a display.

BOXES FOR BOXING DAY

Objective

RE – To think about others.

Group size

Whole class.

What you need

One mini cereal box per child, Christmas wrapping paper, white paper, felt-tipped pens, adhesive tape, glue, a craft knife, photocopied letter (see 'Preparation' below).

Preparation

Send a letter home to parents, saying that the children will be bringing home a small box in which to collect a little money (possibly on Boxing Day) for a local or national named charity. Make it clear that the children must not make a door-to-door collection, and that a few pennies in the box will suffice. Cut out rectangles of white paper (9cm × 6cm), one for each child.

What to do

Let the children cover their boxes with Christmas wrapping paper, securing the edges with adhesive tape. Let each child overwrite, copy or write the name of your chosen charity on the white rectangular pieces of paper, preceded by the word 'For'. Help the children to glue on these 'labels'. When the boxes are covered, an adult may cut a coin slit using a craft knife.

Children could take their boxes home at the beginning of the Christmas holiday, and bring them back on the first day of the Spring Term.

Discussion

Tell the children that the day after Christmas Day is called Boxing Day, probably because on that day a long time ago, charity boxes that had been left in Churches to collect money for poor and ill people were opened, and the money given out. Explain the meaning of the word charity to the children (see also 'St Nicholas' on page 21). Remind the children that both Jesus and St Nicholas gave charity to poor and sick people, and that we should try to do this whenever we can, and especially at Christmas time.

Follow-up activities

✧ Recite the poem 'Wave your hands for Christmas' on page 70. Explain that being kind to people does not only mean giving money, but time, too.
✧ Make contact with a nearby old people's home and ask if there is any appropriate way in which your children may help, for example by giving a short 'concert', or by inviting one or two residents for 'afternoon tea' in your nursery or school and so on.
✧ Ask the children to bring in any outgrown clothes or toys and arrange to take a small group of your children to deliver the items to a local charity shop. If possible, invite a representative of the charity to talk to the children about the work they do.
✧ Recite the poem 'A thinking Christmas' on page 70.

CHAPTER 4
FESTIVE FOOD

In this chapter, children can experiment with an old-fashioned 'Christmas pudding' recipe, make fruit punch and some edible decorations. They learn to work together for everyone's enjoyment.

FRUMENTY

Objective

History — To find out about the origins of 'Christmas pudding'.

Group size

Up to six children.

What you need

Packet of porridge oats, milk, transparent saucepan, wooden spoon, seven saucers, adult access to cooker, tin of prunes, plums, currants, sultanas, raisins, green and black grapes (seedless), cinnamon, nutmeg, honey, breakfast dishes (one per child), teaspoons, a box from a shop-bought Christmas pudding.

Preparation

Cut the plums and grapes into small pieces and put on saucers. Remove a few prunes from the tin, cut up and put on a saucer.

What to do

Tell the children that they are going to make a special kind of Christmas pudding that people used to eat very long ago in the Middle Ages. Say that the pudding was called 'Frumenty' and was made from porridge. Put the oats and milk in the saucepan and follow the packet's instructions; let the children stir in the oats. Heat up the porridge, stirring continuously. When ready, divide the porridge between the children's bowls.

Explain that, at first, 'Frumenty' was also called 'Plum pottage' or 'Plum porridge' because it has small pieces of plum in it. Ask the children if they would like to try this version. Tell the children that some people then decided to put in small pieces of dried plums (prunes), and ask if anyone would like to try this. Explain to them that people then wondered what it would be like to put in small pieces of grapes and also dried grapes (sultanas, currants and raisins). Let the children sprinkle in their own. Explain that people would also put in a little cinnamon, or nutmeg or honey, and let the children do this if they wish. Say that people would also mix in eggs and bake the 'Frumenty' pudding in the oven, and that eventually people decided not to use porridge, but flour instead, to make a 'Christmas pudding' similar to the ones we eat today. Show the children a box from a Christmas pudding, and compare the ingredients with 'Frumenty'.

Discussion

Before the porridge is cooked, do the oats dissolve? Let the children discuss the changes in the porridge, before and after cooking. Can they describe how the cooked porridge would feel? (Set aside a little for this purpose.) Which of the dried fruits came from green or black grapes?

Follow-up activities

✧ Bring in a selection of breakfast cereals with dried fruits and see if the children can name the ingredients.
✧ Teach the rhyme 'Pease pudding' and bring in a tin of 'mushy peas' for the children to try.
✧ Sing the song 'Christmas pud' on page 77.
✧ Let the children tell you about their own inventive 'recipes'. Read extracts from *George's Marvellous Medicine* by Roald Dahl (Puffin).

THE CHRISTMAS TEAM

Objective

Mathematics – To practise one-to-one matching.

Group size

Six children.

What you need

Six each of: mats, plastic plates, plastic tumblers, knives, forks and dessert spoons, paper napkins, replica Christmas crackers (see Preparation below), card, scissors, black felt-tipped pen, adhesive tape, six chairs, one 'group' table, one 'side' table.

Preparation

Make six crackers by rolling crêpe paper into cylinders and winding adhesive tape towards the ends. Make six stand-up name cards, with the first names of the children in the group. On a side table lay out all the items grouped together in sets. Next to this table, put six chairs grouped together. The main table, at which the children will be sitting, should be nearby.

What to do

Explain that parents are often very busy on Christmas day, preparing all the special food for Christmas dinner, and that it would be very helpful if the children could help to set the table. Give each of the children in the 'team' various tasks, for example first child – sets out chairs, second child – place mats and plates, third child – knives, forks and dessert spoons, fourth child – crackers, fifth child – paper napkins, sixth child – name cards and tumblers.

Tell the children that they must all start at the same time, work together and not get in each other's way.

Discussion

How many of you are there? How many place mats, plates, tumblers, knives and so on do you need? How many (items) will you each have? Is there enough of everything? How do you know? Are you counting carefully, 'one at a time'? Have you any (items) left over? Did you have enough or too many? What should you say if you bump into somebody else as you are working? How many people will be coming to Christmas dinner in your family?

Follow-up activities

✧ Once the table has been set let the children sit down and act out eating their Christmas dinner, miming and saying what they are eating and so on.

✧ Invite the children to complete photocopiable page 93. Encourage them to give each bear what they need for Christmas dinner. Can they draw the objects in different sizes for the three bears?

WHAT FOOD?

Objective

Science – To discriminate between different types of Christmas food by smelling and tasting.

Group size

Six to eight children.

What you need

Small dishes of Christmas and other 'universal' food with distinctive tastes and smells, for example Christmas pudding, Brussels sprouts, roast potatoes, bread sauce, redcurrant jelly, turkey, satsumas, chocolate and so on, a blindfold, felt-tipped pen, spoons, somewhere to heat the food, a chart (see 'Preparation' section).

Preparation

Make a chart like the one in the diagram. Check for food allergies, intolerances and vegetarianism.

What to do

Talk about the delicious smell and taste of Christmas food and let the children see the samples. Talk about blind people who have to rely on these senses, plus touch, all the time when they are cooking and eating. Ask the children to take turns to wear a blindfold (or to close their eyes) and try to recognise the Christmas foods by smell and then by taste, using separate spoons for each child. Fill in the charts with the children, by drawing smiley faces on the chart if they recognise the food.

Discussion

What are the children's favourite and least favourite Christmas foods? Why? What do they remind the children of? Can they say which tastes are sweet and which are savoury? Can the children work out which foods have been most easily recognised by smell and by taste by interpreting the chart? Can they think of any other Christmas foods they like?

Follow-up activities

✧ Make up other food charts and experiment to see if the children can recognise different cereals by taste or different fruits by smell.
✧ Taste foods from the festivals of other cultures for example Divali treats, Eid 'Badam Burfi' (almond cakes), Pesach 'Matzah' (unleavened bread) and so on.
✧ Recite the poem 'Christmas mystery' on page 70.
✧ Draw different kinds of food for Santa to eat on his journey, cut out the pictures and put them in a picnic basket for Santa's 'midnight picnic'. Each child can take a turn as Santa, pick out a picture without the others seeing, and describe the food for the others to guess.

Smell Taste

Christmas pudding

Sprouts

Roast potatoes

Bread sauce

Redcurrant jelly

Turkey

Satsumas

Chocolate

Preparation

Cut out holly leaf shapes from the sticky-backed paper. Set out the ingredients, spoon and bowl on a table. Gather the children around you.

What to do

Tell the children they are going to mix a Christmas pudding. Let them share in the adding of the play dough ingredients and take turns to mix. Encourage the children to make some Christmas wishes out loud as they stir.

When each child has had a turn, drop in the 'silver coin' and let the children mould the mixture together into a large 'pudding'. Place this on a plate and add the holly leaves on top.

Choose one child to be the 'grown-up' and to divide the 'pudding' between the four children. Each child then pretends to 'eat' the 'pudding', looking carefully for the 'silver coin'. The child who finds the coin is then allowed to choose or make up a game or song for the group.

Discussion

Tell the children about 'Stir up Sunday', which was four weeks before Christmas, on a Sunday, when people used to stir their Christmas puddings. Each member of the family had a turn to stir and had to make some wishes. Tell the children about the 'game' of finding a silver coin (a 'sixpence') in the pudding, and how some people who found the coin became the 'leader' and chose games or songs for the other people to enjoy.

STIR UP SUNDAY

Objective

English – To think of Christmas wishes, songs and games.

Group size

Up to four children.

What you need

Large plastic bowl, ingredients for play dough (1 cup plain flour, half a cup of salt, 2 teaspoons cream of tartar, 1 cup of water, 2 tablespoons of oil, brown powder paint), green sticky-backed paper, scissors, a large button wrapped in silver foil, large wooden mixing spoon, a large plastic plate, four dishes, four spoons, a serving spoon.

Follow-up activities

✧ Let the children work together to make a Christmas 'plum pie' using play dough pastry, a pie plate and a 'plum' made from a large oval threading bead. Recite the rhyme 'Little Jack Horner', while one child pretends to be Jack, pulling out the plum. Tell the children that there really was a person called Jack Horner, who did have a pie!

✧ Make a graph of the children's favourite puddings.

✧ Draw pictures of Christmas wishes and help the children to write the words underneath.

GOOD ENOUGH TO EAT

Objective

Mathematics — To practise weighing and measuring ingredients.

Group size

Six to eight children.

What you need

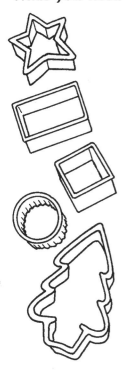

Cutters in Christmas shapes (Christmas tree, star), circle, square and rectangle cutters, a teaspoon, a saucepan, a sieve, weighing scales, three baking trays, a rolling pin, wire cooling racks, 50g of margarine or butter, 50g of soft brown sugar, 1 tablespoon of honey, 225g of plain flour, half a tsp each of mixed spice and bicarbonate of soda and a quarter tsp each of cinnamon and nutmeg, glacé cherries, icing sugar, dried fruit, sugar strands, straws, adult access to an oven, ribbon, aluminium foil.

Preparation

Ensure the children have clean hands. Set out the ingredients, keeping them in their original containers so that the children can 'read' the names on the packets.

What to do

Tell the children they are going to make their own Christmas cookies to hang on their trees. Ask them to help weigh out the sugar, margarine/butter and combine these with the honey in a saucepan. An adult will need to slowly heat the mixture until the fat has melted. After cooling, the children can sieve in the flour and spices to the mixture.

Show the children how to dissolve the bicarbonate of soda in a little water and then add it to the mixture. Let them take turns to knead the mixture and make a dough ball. Wrap the ball in foil and chill it for an hour in the fridge. Set the oven to 375°F/190°C or Gas mark 5. Show the children how to grease three baking trays and roll out the dough onto a floured surface to a _cm thickness.

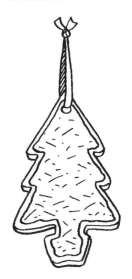

Let the children choose which cutters to use for their individual biscuits. When using the regular shaped cutters, let them name the shapes and see which tessellate and which do not. They can form their initials on their biscuits by pressing in chopped glacé cherries or dried fruit. Ask the children to make a hole in each biscuit using the end of a thick straw (make the hole about 1cm from the top). Bake until golden (about 12-15 minutes) and cool on a wire rack. The children can further decorate the biscuits with icing sugar and sugar strands and thread through the ribbon ready to hang on a tree.

Discussion

Can the children read the scales accurately? Can they understand the concept of 'half a spoon'? Which shapes 'fit together' and which do not? Which shapes leave the most gaps in the biscuit mixture? What can we do with the 'left over' mixture? Can the children identify each other's biscuits by looking at the initials?

Follow-up activities

✧ Make other sorts of Christmas biscuits adding chocolate, ginger, lemon juice and so on. Can the children identify the different flavours?
✧ Practise decorating biscuits using an icing bag with a nozzle.
✧ Recite the poem 'Christmas cookies' on page 69.

EDIBLE SNOW SCENES

Objective

Art – To create 3D snow scenes using edible ingredients.

Group size

Up to six children.

What you need

One paper plate per child, rice paper, icing sugar, water, teaspoons, desiccated coconut, raisins, white marzipan, green food colouring, 'ready to roll' icing, pictures of snowy days.

Preparation

Cut the rice paper into circles, the same size as the paper plates, and then place a rice paper circle on top of each plate. Add a few drops of green food colouring to the marzipan and knead it in, to turn it green. Ensure the children wash their hands thoroughly.

What to do

Let the children discuss the snowy pictures. Explain that they are going to make their own pictures using 'snowy' food. Help the children to mix the icing sugar and water in the small dish to a runny consistency. Let them brush the mixture over their rice paper circles using pastry brushes. Ask them to sprinkle on the desiccated coconut before the icing sugar dries.

Give the children two small pieces of 'ready to roll' icing, to mould into 'ball' shapes to make snowmen. They may use raisins for decoration. Give each child small amounts of green marzipan and help them to make rough triangle shapes as 'fir trees'. The children can now arrange their snowmen and trees on their plates.

Discussion

Talk about the icing sugar before and after the water has been added. Have the children ever tasted freshly fallen snow? What did it taste like? Can you make the sprinkled coconut look like a light snowfall and then a heavy snowfall? Do the children know that a fir tree is called an 'evergreen' tree? Do they know why?

Follow-up activities

✧ Mould marzipan into Father Christmas shapes, using red food colouring for his clothes.
✧ Bring in a whole coconut and break it in half for the children to see coconut in its natural state. Taste some!
✧ Ask the children to bring in some domed 'snowstorm' scenes for a collection. Make one by sticking a small plastic snowman to the bottom of a jam jar with strong glue. When the glue is dry, fill the jar with water and add tiny pieces of aluminium foil as 'snowflakes'. Screw on the lid, and gently shake the jar.

MELTING SNOWMEN

Objective

Science — To observe the effect of warmth on ice-cream 'snow'.

Group size

Six to eight children.

What you need

Ice-cream scoop, ice-cream, small piece of carrot, chocolate buttons, red liquorice, raisins, a large plate, spoons, a tray, pictures of snowmen.

Preparation

Make sure that the ice cream is well frozen at the beginning of the activity. Set out the chocolate buttons, raisins, liquorice and carrot on the tray.

What to do

Look at the snowmen pictures and say that the children are going to make some from ice-cream. Scoop out two balls of ice-cream and place them one on top of the other to form a snowman on the plate. Let the children carefully, but quickly, decorate it with chocolate buttons, red liquorice for the mouth, carrot nose and raisin eyes. Leave it in a sunny spot of the classroom and make observations every few minutes. Let the children taste the melted mixture.

Discussion

What do you think will happen to the 'snowman'? Why will it melt and how long do you think it will take? How would you feel if you built a snowman and it melted? Does the snowman still taste of ice-cream when it has melted? Would a bigger snowman take longer to melt? What happens to snow when it melts? What does it turn into? How is ice-cream like snow? Where do we keep ice-cream? Why?

Follow-up activities

✧ Talk about the book *The Snowman* by Raymond Briggs (Picture Puffin) and watch the video. Sit the children in a circle and let each child have a turn to say 'If the Snowman came into my house we would ...'.

✧ Draw pictures of 'The Snowman' on card, cover with glue and cotton wool and then cut him out. Ask each child to draw and cut out a picture of him or herself on card. Stick the two figures side by side with adhesive tape, and stick a piece of invisible thread to the back of the head of each figure, then suspend them from the ceiling to make it look as if the child and 'The Snowman' are 'walking in the air'.

✧ Let the children make a simple zigzag book in five sections, showing a full snowman, then the snowman 'a quarter gone', then 'half gone', 'three quarters gone', and finally, a puddle to depict that the snowman has 'all gone'.

✧ On a snowy day, make a real snowman and time how long it takes to melt. Alternatively, bring two sweet jars full of snow inside for observation. Put one on a sunny windowsill and the other somewhere fairly cool.

HERE WE COME A WASSAILING!

Objective

Mathematics – To practise measuring liquid.

Group size

Four children.

What you need

An apple, an orange, a knife, a ladle, two cups of apple juice, two cups of pineapple juice, 1 cup of blackcurrant drink, a lemon, $\frac{1}{2}$ teaspoon of cinnamon, 3 teaspoons of brown sugar, 250ml of ginger ale, a large bowl, a large pan, plastic tumblers, plastic cups, a measuring jug, a lemon squeeze, teaspoons, adult access to a cooker.

Preparation

Slice the apple and orange and sprinkle with lemon juice, to float in the punch later.

What to do

Tell the children that a 'punch' is a mixture of different drinks, and that a long time ago people enjoyed making punches for Christmas called 'Wassail' which means 'Be well!'. Let the children taste the different juices before they are mixed into the punch. Help the children measure the right amount of ginger ale, using a measuring jug, and to pour it into the pan.

They should then count the cupfuls of juice as they pour them in the pan. Help the children to squeeze the lemon and to pour it into the pan, before adding the cinnamon and sugar.

Heat the punch gently until it is almost boiling and leave to cool. When the punch has cooled, add the fruit slices. Let the children take turns to ladle the punch into tumblers for one another, taking care to 'scoop' up the fruit slices. Ask the children to say whether they want a 'full' or a 'half' tumbler of punch.

Discussion

Can the children taste the individual juices in the punch? Ask the children what other warm drinks they like to have, and when. Ask the children to think of happy, 'warm' words to describe how warm drinks make them feel.

Follow-up activities

✧ Make a bar chart to show the children's favourite warm drinks, and one of their cold drinks.

✧ Bring in small packets of fruit juices and the 'matching' fresh fruits, and see if the children can relate them.

✧ Cover a table with a plastic cloth and place on it a small washing-up bowl, three-quarters full of water. Give each child a tall transparent beaker. Each child throws a dice, and depending on the number thrown, pours the corresponding number of small cupfuls of water into their beaker. The winner is the child with the most water when the four beakers are lined up.

CHAPTER 5
FUN AND GAMES

Christmas is a time for enjoyment and this chapter provides ideas for singing, acting and dancing all on the festive theme.

THE SOUNDS OF CHRISTMAS

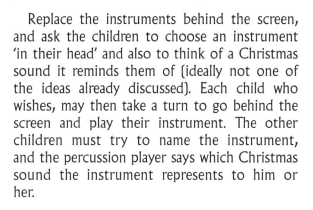

Objective

Music — To identify percussion instruments, when played out of sight.

Group size

Up to six children.

What you need

Selection of percussion instruments, a 'screen' (for example, puppet theatre or curtain on washing line and so on), a small table.

Preparation

Set out the instruments on a table, behind the screen.

What to do

Sit the children in a circle. Hold up the instruments one at a time and play them. See if the children can name them, and say what sort of Christmas sounds each instrument reminds them of. For example, wood blocks — crackers or balloons 'popping'; two chimes on glockenspiel — visitors ringing a doorbell, triangle — clock chiming that it is time to eat Christmas dinner; sleigh bells — Santa's reindeers; sandpaper blocks — feet trudging through snow; drum beat — snow falling off roof with a thud.

Replace the instruments behind the screen, and ask the children to choose an instrument 'in their head' and also to think of a Christmas sound it reminds them of (ideally not one of the ideas already discussed). Each child who wishes, may then take a turn to go behind the screen and play their instrument. The other children must try to name the instrument, and the percussion player says which Christmas sound the instrument represents to him or her.

Discussion

What sort of sounds do you hear in the morning, afternoon and night-time at Christmas time? Which sounds are loud and soft? Which sounds make you feel happy, sad or cross? Why? What are your favourite Christmas songs and carols? What sort of music do you like to dance to at Christmas parties?

Follow-up activities

✧ Make a bar chart of favourite Christmas songs and carols.
✧ Adapt the carol 'We Wish You a Merry Christmas' with words based on the five senses for example 'We Wish You the Sound Of Sleigh Bells', 'We Wish You the Smell of Mince Pies' and so on.
✧ Read the story 'Baboushka' on page 85. Discuss how to make appropriate 'sound effects' with the children. Make a tape recording of the story with the children making the sound effects.
✧ Using percussion instruments and voices, make up a Christmas sound song, based on the tune of the first line of 'Here we go round the Mulberry Bush', for example 'This is the sound my Dad's drill / my new puppy dog / my baby doll / makes...'.

THE DOLLS' CHRISTMAS

Objective

Art – To decorate a dolls' house for Christmas.

Group size

Up to four children.

What you need

A dolls' house, furniture, play people, coloured tissue circles, a hole punch, string, scissors, adhesive tape, coloured, gummed paper, tinsel, tiny sprig of Christmas tree branch, Blu-Tack, cotton wool, used Christmas cards which show decorations, wrapping paper.

Preparation

Cut the string into pieces, each 30cm long. Knot one end of each piece, and wrap a small amount of adhesive tape around the other end to make a 'threading' end. Punch a hole in the middle of the tissue circles. Cut the gummed paper into small strips to make miniature paper chains.

What to do

Let the children look at Christmas cards and wrapping paper for ideas about decorations. Next show them how to thread the string through the tissue circles, and help them to hang up the string in the dolls' house, along with lengths of tinsel. Help the children as necessary to make paper chains from the strips of gummed paper, and to hang these in the house.

Help the children to decorate a miniature 'Christmas tree' made from a tiny sprig stuck in Blu-Tack. Finally, let the children cover the roof with cotton wool 'snow' and arrange the furniture and play people inside the house.

Discussion

What kinds of decorations do you have in your house at Christmas? Do you help to make any or put them up? Do you make any decorations for relatives and friends? Do you have any decorations on your tree that you can eat? What do you put at the top of your Christmas tree? Where do you keep your decorations after Christmas? What kinds of decorations have you seen in other people's houses?

Follow-up activities

✧ Let the children cut out pictures of furniture from catalogues and stick them on paper to make 'room' pictures and add 'Christmas decorations' using felt-tipped pens, gummed and crêpe paper, tinsel and so on.
✧ Sing the song 'Paper chains' on page 79, and learn the actions together.
✧ Tell the children how, long ago before shops sold decorations, people used holly, ivy, mistletoe and privet to decorate their houses. Talk about why these are called 'evergreens', and bring in samples to add to the decorations in the dolls' house. Ask if the children's homes are decorated with these at Christmas.

DAY AND NIGHT

Objective

Science – To distinguish between day and night-time Christmas activities.

Group size

Up to eight children.

What you need

A dice, six small, sticky labels, a piece of pale blue A2 card, a piece of dark blue A2 card, used Christmas cards, Blu-Tack, cotton wool, silver foil, felt-tipped pens, a tray.

Preparation

Stick labels onto each face of the dice. On three of them draw a moon and stars, and on the other three some clouds and sun. Stick some cotton wool 'clouds' at the top of the pale blue paper to represent 'day-time'. Cut out a foil moon and stick this at the top of the dark blue paper to represent 'night-time'. Affix the two large pieces of paper to the wall, side-by-side, at child height.

Sift through the cards, looking for those depicting a day-time or night-time Christmas activity and cut the pictures from the cards. Put a selection of the cards in the tray on the floor, in front of the two wall pictures and sit the children in a semi-circle around the tray.

What to do

Talk about what happens in the day and at night-time during Christmas time, such as Santa delivering presents at night and eating Christmas dinner in the day and so on. Give one child in turn the dice to throw. Depending on whether the dice lands on 'day' or 'night', the child must select an appropriate card from the tray, say what is happening, and stick it on either the 'day' or 'night' wall picture.

Discussion

What sort of things do you do during the day at Christmas time? What do you like best and why? As each child sticks their picture on either the 'day' or 'night' large picture, ask why that activity would not normally take place at the opposite end of the day (for example, why do people not usually build snowmen at night!).

Follow-up activities

✧ Each child in the semi-circle begins a sentence with 'On Christmas Eve I like to …', or 'On Christmas Day I like to …'.
✧ Ask the children to complete the photocopiable sheet on page 94, drawing either clouds or stars 'in the sky' or 'through the window', to show whether the activities normally occur during the day or at night.

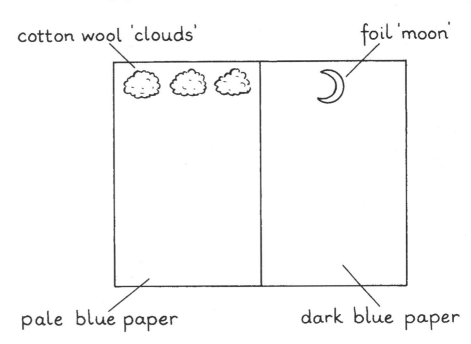

cotton wool 'clouds'   foil 'moon'

pale blue paper   dark blue paper

CHRISTMAS FACES

Objective

English – To talk about 'Christmas Day feelings'.

Group size

Up to six children.

What you need

Four paper plates, four kitchen roll tubes, adhesive tape, felt-tipped pens, miniature 'discussion' items (or pictures), for example a Christmas parcel, a tree, a card in an envelope, a balloon, 'Christmas' food, a snowman, a cracker, a dog, a television and so on, a draw-string bag.

Preparation

Draw faces on the plates to show the expressions - happy, sad, cross and surprised. Stick a kitchen roll tube to each plate with adhesive tape so that the children can hold the plates up in front of their own faces. Put the miniature items and pictures in the bag. Arrange the children round the table, or in a circle on the floor, with the 'faces' in the centre.

What to do

Tell the children that Christmas Day is so exciting and busy that we can feel happy, sad, surprised and even a little cross, all in one day! Hold up the 'faces', and ask the children to describe the expressions. Say that you are going to put your hand in the bag and hold up an object or picture and one of the masks, and that you will make up a little story about it, beginning, 'On Christmas Day I felt ...'. For example, bring out the dog, hold up the 'cross' mask and say, 'On Christmas Day I felt cross because my dog tore up some decorations.' Now pass the bag to each child in turn and let them develop the idea.

Discussion

What kinds of things do you do that make your family feel happy/sad/cross or surprised? Why do you think they feel like that? What kinds of exciting things happen on Christmas Day that are special on that day?

Follow-up activities

✧ Play 'Pass the expression', in which children in a circle 'pass round' different facial expressions for example, a smile, a frown and so on.
✧ Let the children pick a doll or soft toy and decide on its facial expression, and make up a simple story about it.
✧ Read the story 'Mole's best Christmas' on page 86, and ask one child to hold up a 'face' at the appropriate points in the story.

rope, a football, a bicycle, a slide, a trampoline, a pair of scissors, a book, a baby doll and so on).

What to do

Recite the following rhyme with the children:
Early in the morning
At eight o'clock
I can hear the postperson knock
He (she) gives me a parcel
I open it up
Early in the morning at eight o'clock!

Sit the children in a circle on the floor. Choose one child to be the postperson and wear the cap and jacket. Put one of the picture cards inside the box and give the box to the 'postperson'. Ask the children to recite the rhyme again as the 'postperson' walks around the edge of the circle, carrying the box. At the end of the rhyme, the 'postperson' stops behind a child and gives the box to the child. The child takes out the picture and mimes using the 'present'. The other children must guess what the 'present' is.

Discussion

Why can't a postperson put a parcel through the letter box? Have you ever received a parcel through the post? What was in the parcel, and who sent it? How do you think a postperson would feel carrying a very heavy parcel? What do you think happens if no one is at home to receive the parcel?

Follow-up activities

✧ Play 'Kim's game', putting three or more 'present' pictures on a tray. Ask a child to look at the pictures, then close their eyes while you remove one. See if the child can guess which one is missing.
✧ Ask the children to think of gifts to send to characters in stories and nursery rhymes, for example Little Red Riding Hood or Jack in Jack and Jill and so on.
✧ Give the children catalogues and ask them to cut out pictures of Christmas presents. Make labels saying 'toy box', 'wardrobe', 'chest of drawers' and so on and ask the children to 'tidy the presents away' by putting the pictures under the appropriate labels.

GIFTS GALORE!

Objective

PE – To mime the actions involved in using Christmas gifts.

Group size

Up to eight children.

What you need

A box (approximately 20cm × 20cm) with a top 'lid', Christmas wrapping paper, adhesive tape, scissors, card, felt-tipped pens, a postperson's cap and jacket, floor space.

Preparation

Cover the box in the wrapping paper, securing it with adhesive tape. Ensure that the top 'lid' can easily be lifted up and down. Cut the card into rectangles each approximately 14cm × 10cm, and on each piece of card draw a picture of a Christmas gift, the use of which can be obviously mimed by the children (a skipping

TWELVE DAYS OF CHRISTMAS

Objective

Mathematics — To practise sequencing the numbers 1 to 12.

Group size

Twelve children, with the rest of the group watching.

What you need

Twelve 'A4' cards, ribbon, a hole punch, felt-tipped pens, book(s) illustrating the song 'The Twelve Days of Christmas', two calendars — one for the current year and one for the 'New Year', twelve chairs.

Preparation

Draw the numbers 1st, 2nd, 3rd and so on, up to 12th, on each of the A4 cards. Punch two holes at the top of each card and thread ribbon through so that the cards can be worn like a 'necklace'. Sing the song with the children and show them the illustrations in the book(s). Show the children when the twelve days of Christmas occur, pointing to the days in the two calendars (start counting on Boxing Day and end on 6 January).

What to do

Give each of the twelve children a 'necklace' to wear. Depending on their number ask them to draw a relevant picture to go on their card (partridge, turtle doves and so on). Now ask them to line themselves up 'in order'. When they have done this, let them sit on a row of chairs, side by side.

Sing the song again, all together, and as each 'day' is mentioned, the appropriate child must stand up.

Discussion

Ask what presents were given on the 'first' and 'last' days of Christmas, and on the 'middle' day of the Christmas holiday period. Explain that the twelfth day of Christmas is 6 January, and that is when people believe that the three Kings visited Jesus. Say that many people like to take down their Christmas decorations by 6 January.

Follow-up activities

✧ Ask the children how many presents the person in the song received altogether on the 'second/third day of Christmas' and so on.
✧ Make simple 'lift the flap', Advent-type calendars showing numbers to 12, with 'presents' underneath the flaps.

CHRISTMAS RHYME TIME

Objective

English – To be aware of Christmas rhyming words.

Group size

Four children.

What you need

Card, scissors, felt-tipped pens, old Christmas cards, magazines, glue.

Preparation

Cut the cards into twenty four 'playing cards' (18cm × 12cm). On twelve of the cards, draw the

following 'Christmas' pictures (or use pictures from old cards and magazines) – a Christmas tree, Santa Claus, a sack, a sleigh, snow, a bell, a star, a paper chain, a (gift) box, a balloon, the three Kings, a (woolly) hat. Draw a capital 'C' in the top right hand corner of each card. On the other twelve cards, draw (or stick) the following pictures, each to rhyme with one of the pictures in the previous set - a bee, two doors, a 'blob' of black, a tray, a bow, a shell, a car, some rain, a fox, a spoon, some rings, a cat. Sit the children round the table. Split the cards into two sets, the 'Christmas' cards (each with the capital 'C') and the 'non-Christmas' cards.

What to do

Tell the children that at Christmas time, we sing lots of songs, say poems and read cards with rhyming words in them. Read some of the verses in the cards to the children, and sing some Christmas carols and songs to demonstrate. Give out three 'non-Christmas' cards to each child, keeping the 'Christmas' ones yourself. Hold one up, and ask who has a rhyming card. The first child to collect three pairs of rhyming cards is the 'winner'.

Discussion

Do you know any nursery rhymes or pop songs with rhymes in them? Do you know any funny rhymes? Do you ever make up any 'nonsense' rhymes? Why do you think babies like baby rhymes?

Follow-up activities

✧ Recite the poem 'Questions on Christmas Eve' on page 68, a few times. Pause just before the last word on the second line of each pair of rhyming couplets to see if the children can supply the rhyme.
✧ Sing carols and songs, and let children take turns to bang a drum each time they hear a 'rhyme'.
✧ Mix up the 'Christmas' and 'non-Christmas' cards, and give three cards to each child in a group of four to play 'I-spy'. Each time a child correctly matches his or her card with your initial sound, the child covers the card with a counter until all three cards are covered.

MUSICAL CHRISTMAS BOXES

Objective

Music – To lead a group in singing Christmas carols and songs.

Group size

Five children.

What you need

Five boxes with lids, card, scissors, felt-tipped pens, a cassette recorder, a cassette of Christmas music and songs (suitable for dancing), a chair, floor space.

Preparation

Cut the cards into five rectangles which will fit inside the boxes (approximately 12cm × 8cm). On each card, draw a picture to denote a Christmas carol or song known by the children, for example baby Jesus in a manger for 'Away in a Manger', three Kings for 'We Three Kings', some shepherds for 'While Shepherds Watched', a reindeer for 'Rudolph the Red-nosed Reindeer' and some sleigh bells for 'Jingle Bells'. Place a card inside each box and arrange the boxes on the floor, with space between for the children to dance a r o u n d them.

What to do

Tell the children that they are going to play a game similar to 'musical chairs', called 'Musical Christmas boxes'. Ask the children to dance to the music, taking care not to bump into the boxes. When the music stops, each child must sit on the floor and pick up the box nearest to them. Sit the children in a circle and let each one, in turn, open their box, look at the picture and try to guess the name of the carol or song. The children then join together to sing the carol or song.

Discussion

Talk about how Christmas songs about Jesus are called 'carols'. What are your favourite carols? How do they make you feel when you sing them? What 'pictures do you see in your head' when you sing the words? Have you ever been carol-singing or to a carol concert?

Follow-up activities

✧ Teach the children how to clap out the rhythms to well-known carols and songs. Let them take turns to clap out rhythms for others to guess.

✧ Write out the words of familiar carols and songs in a big book, and let the children 'read' the words, using the technique described in 'Nativity rebus' on page 12.

✧ Give the children Christmas cards to look at, and ask them to suggest carols or songs to 'match' the cards.

CHAPTER 6
CHRISTMAS AROUND THE WORLD

In this chapter children learn, through games, art, design and technology, and science activities, how other people celebrate Christmas.

PÈRE NOEL

Objective

History – To learn about the French tradition of 'Father Christmas'.

Group size

Up to eight children.

What you need

A 'Santa' hat, a hobby horse, a metre rule or a garden cane, string, scissors, two small baskets, a carrot, a pair of baby's shoes, a pair of children's shoes, a pair of adult's shoes, a baby's rattle, a bib, a bucket and spade, an adult-sized scarf, an adult-sized woollen hat, a pair of coconut shells, a map of the world, floor space.

Preparation

Tie the ruler lengthwise across the hobby horse, just below the head. Tie the baskets on to the ends of the ruler. Put the rattle, bib and spade in one basket. Divide the rattle, bib, bucket, spade, scarf and woollen hat between the two baskets, putting a mixture of 'baby', 'children's' and 'grown-up' gifts in each basket.

What to do

Point out France on the map. Explain that in France, 'Father Christmas' is called 'Père Noel', and that people say he rides on a donkey on Christmas Eve to deliver presents. Say that French people leave out a pair of shoes, instead of stockings, for 'Père Noel' to fill with presents. Say that they also leave out a carrot for the donkey.

Ask one child to choose a pair of shoes to 'leave out' for 'Père Noel' with the carrot. Choose another child to be 'Père Noel' wearing the 'Santa' hat and riding on the hobby horse 'donkey'. Let another child play the coconut shells as 'sound effects'. When 'Père Noel' sees the shoes 'he' must decide whether they belong to a baby, child or a 'grown-up'. 'Père Noel' then selects two appropriate gifts from his baskets (for example the bucket and spade) and places them on top of the shoes. 'He' picks up the carrot and 'feeds' it to the donkey. Another child is then chosen to be 'Père Noel'.

Discussion

Ask the children for their ideas on other gifts suitable for a baby, a child and a 'grown-up'. Ask what other food a donkey might like to eat. What do the children leave out for Santa's reindeers?

Follow-up activities

✧ Teach the children to say 'Joyeux Noel' to one another.
✧ Make small, wrapped 'parcels', and let the children give them to one another. Teach the children to thank each other by saying *'Merci beaucoup'*.

PINATA

Objective

PE – To respond to spoken signals when blindfolded.

Group size

Up to six children.

What you need

A blindfold or scarf, washing line, small shallow decorative basket, aluminium foil, tinsel, crêpe paper in various colours, sugar paper, scissors, small round bat, a map of the world, paper, a pencil.

Preparation

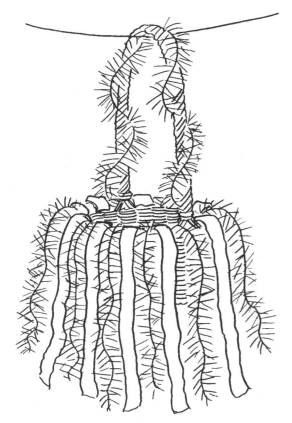

Roll the foil loosely into ten balls, each roughly the size of a tennis ball. Cut the crêpe paper into 'streamers', approximately 30cm long. Cut the tinsel into pieces the same length as the crêpe paper. Attach the 'streamers' and tinsel to the basket. Thread the washing line through the handle of the basket and suspend the line.

Cut out a square of sugar paper (40cm × 40cm).

What to do

Point out Mexico on the map and tell the children about the Mexican game of Pinata, in which a blindfolded child uses a stick to try and break an earthenware pot, decorated with streamers and tinsel and hung from the ceiling. When the pot is broken the sweets inside fall on the ground and are shared out.

Blindfold a willing child and ask another to move the basket along the line to a spot of their choice and put the foil balls inside. Ask another child to place the sugar paper square on the floor near to the basket. Tell the children that they must help the blindfolded child to find the square by saying the words 'hot' or 'cold' - 'hot' as the child moves near to the square and 'cold' as the child moves away. Once the child has found the square and stood on it, remove the blindfold and give the child the bat. The child then gently hits the basket, making the balls fall out. Each child is allowed only one 'hit' per turn unless they 'miss' the basket entirely. The child counts the fallen balls and writes down the number. The winner is the child who knocks out the most balls.

Discussion

Ask each blindfolded child how it felt not to be able to see. Talk about how blind people have to listen very carefully to sounds around them, especially traffic. What sounds can you hear at pedestrian crossings? How might they help a blind person?

Follow-up activities

✧ Arrange dolls' houses on the floor, covered in cotton wool 'snow'. Say there is a 'blizzard' and Father Christmas cannot see very well because of the snow, and needs help to find the chimneys. One child holds up a miniature Father Christmas in his 'sleigh', while another holds a play person at a window and directs Father Christmas to their house.
✧ Play the traditional party game of 'Hot and cold', in which these words are used to help a child find a hidden object.

MARTIN'S TREE

Objective

Art – To create a group picture of a Christmas forest in 'silhouette'.

Group size

Four children at a time.

What you need

A4 sheet of black sugar paper, dark blue art paper, tinsel, scissors, glue, white wax crayons, a map of the world.

Preparation

Cut the tinsel into pieces 3cm long. Stick together the pieces of dark blue paper to make a background, approximately 100cm × 80cm.

What to do

Tell the children the story of how people think the first Christmas tree was 'invented'. Point out Germany on the map and tell the children that a famous man called Martin Luther was born there a long time ago. Say that one night he was walking home through a forest of tall fir trees and saw lots of stars twinkling through the branches. These made Martin think of the stars that twinkled over Bethlehem when Jesus was born, and he thought that the stars looked like lights shining on the trees. When he arrived home, he brought in a small fir tree from his garden and tied candles to the branches. When he carefully lit the candles, they reminded Martin of the stars twinkling in the forest, and he called his tree a 'Christmas' tree.

Tell the children that they can work together to make a large picture of 'Martin's forest'. Let each child draw a tree on the black paper, cut it out and stick it on the blue background. Let the children stick the tinsel at the ends of the 'branches', to look as though they are stars twinkling through the trees.

Discussion

Ask the children if they have ever been out at night. What colour was everything? Talk about 'silhouettes'. Do the children ever think that objects in their bedrooms look like other things in the dark? Talk about how it is very dangerous to use real candles on a Christmas tree and how, long ago, lots of trees caught fire. For this reason, people kept a bowl of water near their trees. Talk about how, today, we use electric 'fairy lights' instead. Reinforce the fact that only grown-ups must touch them.

Follow-up activities

✧ Use a large torch or table lamp and white paper, and let the children experiment with shadow making.

SNOW OR SUN?

Objective

Geography – To make comparisons between two countries.

Group size

Six children.

What you need

A globe of the world, two pieces of card (60cm × 42cm), adhesive tape, scissors, cotton wool, glue, felt-tipped pens, white paper.

Preparation

Stick the two large pieces of card together and draw a line down the middle. Stick small cotton wool balls at the top of the left-hand side to represent snow and write 'United Kingdom' underneath. Draw a sun at the top of the right-hand side and write 'Australia'. Cut the white paper into rectangles, each approximately 15cm × 10cm.

What to do

Explain that Christmas is celebrated in December by people in countries all over the world. Tell the children that in some countries, such as the United Kingdom, it is winter time, and likely to snow, and that in other countries, such as Australia, it is summer time in December, and will be hot. Point out the UK and Australia on the globe.

Talk about how Christmas is celebrated in a cold country, and ask the children how they think Christmas is celebrated in a hot country. (See also 'Discussion' below.) Ask the children to each draw a picture of either a 'UK' or 'Australian' Christmas. When they have finished, ask them to turn their pictures over, put them in the middle of the table and mix them up. Each child must choose a picture and decide whether it is a picture of the UK or Australia, and then stick it on the correct side of the large card.

Discussion

Ask the children what kinds of things they do, eat and wear in the summer. Ask them to imagine doing some of these things to celebrate Christmas. Tell them that in Australia, for example, people cook their turkeys on barbecues and eat Christmas pudding and mince pies at the beach. Ask the children what clothes they think Santa might wear in Australia.

Follow-up activities

✧ Read the poem 'Sunny Santa' on page 71, and ask the children to draw Santa in his 'Australian' clothes.

✧ Read the poem 'Is it cold at Christmas?' on page 71. Talk about Lapland, 'the land of the midnight sun', where it is 'always dark' in winter, and 'always light' in summer.

✧ Sort 'hot' and 'cold' clothes into sets.

CHRISTMAS VISITORS

Objective

Geography — To talk about distances and appropriate forms of travel.

Group size

Four children.

What you need

Five A4 pieces of card, card, scissors, felt-tipped pens, 16 play figures, miniature transport vehicles (4 each of aeroplanes, train engines and cars), a building-block cube, adhesive tape, a tray, a map of the world, a map of the British Isles, a street map of your local area.

Preparation

Draw this diagram onto one of the A4 pieces of card and then photocopy it three times onto the other pieces of card:

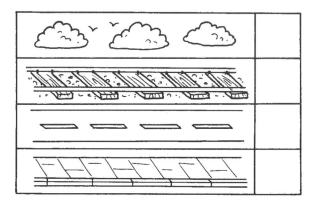

On the remaining piece of card, draw round the cube six times. Cut out the six squares and illustrate each one:

Stick the squares on each side of the cube with adhesive tape to make a 'dice'. Display the

world and British Isles maps where they will be visible to the children as they sit round a table. Cut some card into four pieces (each 5cm × 2cm). Draw a pair of shoes on each piece. Put the vehicles, 'shoe cards' and play people on a tray.

What to do

Point out various countries and places known to the children on the world and British Isles maps, and talk about the forms of transport we use to get to and from these places. Talk about visitors who travel 'on foot', and show the children their own streets and so on, on the local map.

Give each child a card and say that they are expecting four Christmas visitors: one travelling by air, one by rail, one by road and one 'on foot'. Each child throws the 'dice' and depending on how it lands, selects the appropriate 'vehicle' (including the 'shoes') from the tray, together with a play figure. The child places the 'vehicle' on the appropriate part of their card, and the play person in the right hand space.

Encourage the children to make up a little 'story' about each play person, thinking up a name and saying where the person is travelling from - a different country, a place in the British Isles or from within walking distance of their home. The first child to 'cover' their card with an aeroplane, engine, car, 'shoes' and four visitors, is the winner of the game.

Discussion

Talk about places that the children have visited. Are they going to see anyone at Christmas? How will they get there? What do they enjoy about journeys, and what do they dislike? Who is coming to visit them?

Follow-up activities

✧ Sing the song 'Sharing Christmas' on page 80.
✧ Use the idea on page 62 and make a display of the children's families at Christmas.
✧ Read the poem 'The Christmas tree lights' on page 71.

THE BIRDS' CHRISTMAS EVE

Objective

Science – To make a bird cake.

Group size

Four children.

What you need

Half a block of vegetable fat, saucepan, cooker, kitchen scraps (cheese, fruit, crumbs and so on), margarine tub, awl, string, a map of the world, bird seed, wooden spoon, a dessert spoon.

Preparation

Make two holes in the margarine tub just under the rim, and thread the string through so that the tub may be hung in the garden.

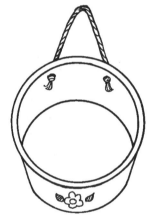

What to do

Tell the children about how the countries of Norway, Denmark and Sweden are called Scandinavia, and point them out on the map. Tell the children that on Christmas Eve the Scandinavian people very kindly remember to give a present to birds. On Christmas Eve they put out some food for the birds, such as a bird cake, in their gardens.

Show the children the ingredients, including the block of fat. Put it in the pan and then gently heat it until it melts. Remove from the cooker. Under careful supervision, let the children take turns to mix in the scraps (use $\frac{1}{3}$ fat to $\frac{2}{3}$ scraps and seeds). Do not use peanuts because of the danger of choking or allergic reaction in young children. Allow the mixture to cool. Let the children spoon the mixture into the margarine tub, press it down firmly and allow to solidify. Take the 'cake' into the

garden and hang it accessibly for the birds. (If possible leave out a small dish of water for them too.)

Discussion

What do birds like to eat? What is the best way of mixing all these ingredients together? How can we make this hard block go soft? What does it need to make it melt? What do you think will happen to the mixture now that everything is mixed together? Do you ever leave out food for the birds? Do you know the names of any birds you see? Why should we leave out food for birds in winter time?

Follow-up activities

✧ Ask the children to make a Christmas card for a pet known to them (or an animal in a story).
✧ Talk about Christmas presents for pets, and ask the children to complete the photocopiable sheet on page 95 by joining the pets and gifts with a line.

A TABLE STABLE

Objective

Design and Technology – To make a stable underneath a table.

Group size

Four children at a time.

What you need

A small table, large sheets of card, adhesive tape, white paper, paints, glue, scissors, felt-tipped pens, washing-up liquid bottles, small amount of dry sand, funnel, fabric scraps, ribbon, a small food carton for a 'manger', a small doll for 'baby Jesus', straw (from pet shop), a map of the world.

Preparation

Cut the card to size to make 'walls' for the stable. Cut the card into ovals for faces of the figures in the stable.

What to do

Tell the children about the Polish custom of creating a nativity stable underneath a table, and point out Poland on the map. Help the children, as necessary, to stick 'walls' around three sides of the stable. If they wish, they may want to stick two pieces of card at the front (each piece of card attached down one side with adhesive tape to a table leg) to make two large 'doors', which may be opened to reveal the scene inside.

Let the children paint some animals on white paper, cut them out when dry and stick them to the three walls to form the background. Help the children to funnel a small amount of dry sand into the washing-up liquid bottles to make them steady. Ask the children to draw faces on the card ovals and to stick them on the washing-up liquid bottles, adding fabric scraps for clothes. Paint a small food carton as a manger and put a small doll inside as baby Jesus. Use large sheets of card for a floor and sprinkle a little straw on it.

Discussion

How many walls should the stable have? What will the front be like? Do you want it to be left open or have two big doors? How shall we fix them to the stable? What kinds of animals would you like to paint along the walls, and how many will there be room for? How many people do you want to put in the stable? How can we stop the washing-up liquid bottles from wobbling? What do you think it would be like to stay in a stable? Do you think you would like it? Why?

Follow-up activities

✧ Let the children make their own simple 'stables' from construction sets, play people, farm animal sets and so on.
✧ Read the poem 'One, two, three' on page 67.

A TREE FROM NORWAY

Objective

Art – To make a mural of a giant Christmas tree.

Group size

Up to eight children.

What you need

A roll of wallpaper, scissors, paints, sponges, small dishes, brushes, sheets of art paper in various colours (including dark blue), adhesive tape, white paper, silver glitter, glue, floor space, a map of the world.

Preparation

Decide how tall you can make your tree (floor to ceiling, if possible). Cut three lengths of wallpaper accordingly. Roll them in the opposite direction to flatten them and stick the lengths together, side-by-side, with adhesive tape on the printed side. Carefully turn the wallpaper over onto the plain side and secure the corners with heavy objects to keep it flat. Draw a Christmas tree shape, leaving enough space at the top, bottom and round the sides to enable children to kneel on the wallpaper and sponge-print the inside of the tree shape, with-out getting paint on the floor surface. Cut out the white paper into tulip-shaped 'lights'. Cut enough to decorate the tree. Attach enough dark blue art paper to the wall as background.

What to do

Tell the children that every year the people of Norway very kindly send an enormous Christmas tree to the people of Great Britain. This tree is put on a ship and sent across the North Sea to Felixstowe, where it is put on a huge transporter and taken to Trafalgar Square in London. Point out Norway, the North Sea and the approximate positions of Felixstowe and London on the map. Tell the children that the people of the British Isles have built a rose garden in Oslo, in Norway, to say thank you for all the lovely trees.

To make your Christmas tree, let four children sponge-print the tree in green paint, while another four children put glue on the white 'lights' and sprinkle them with silver glitter. While the tree is drying, let another eight children draw, paint and cut out buildings and people. When the tree is dry, stick on the 'lights'. When the glue has dried, cut out the tree and attach it to the dark blue background paper. Add the buildings and people.

coat with glue and sprinkle with silver glitter

Discussion

Talk about how the people of Norway always decorate their tree with white lights. Ask the children about their tree decorations. How would the tree be moved onto the ship, and onto the transporter? Have the children seen any large trees in 'squares', shopping centres and so on nearby?

Follow-up activities

✧ on the carpet, using a big 'ship', a transporter, buildings and play people.
✧ Let the children draw pictures of the tree on the ship and on the transporter.

CHAPTER 7
DISPLAYS

This chapter gives general ideas for making interactive displays to encourage discussion and teamwork, as well as ideas for four specific displays on the Christmas theme.

INTRODUCTION

A display can present excellent opportunities to encourage discussion among the children, as they plan, talk about the display in the preparation stage, devise new ways of using it over a period of time and explain it to parents and visitors. Involve the children at every stage, to encourage co-operation and team work.

To encourage the children to use and talk about all their senses, use a wide variety of resources, both natural and manufactured. Include interesting textures, especially from 'found' objects, smells and tastes. Hardware and gardening stores can provide a wealth of ideas.

Make displays three-dimensional, by using tables, shelving and so on to project the display 'outwards' from a wall, to encourage the children to 'touch and talk'.

Consider using a set of bookshelves, together with sets of play figures and a 'background' made from appropriate wallpaper, wrapping paper or pictures painted by the children to create a scene (a home at Christmas). Transform the wallpapered shelves into rooms using dolls' house furniture, play people, and decorations. Alternatively, recreate a 'snowy day' using cars, play people, buildings made from small bricks, cotton wool 'snow', an 'icy pond' mirror, a background of 'snowy' trees and so on.

Extend the learning opportunities and usefulness of a display by making more than one set of labels for the children to place next to the appropriate object. For example in addition to naming labels, try colour words, numerals, speech bubbles and feelings (happy, sad and so on).

wallpaper strips

cut out figures

WHAT DID THEY SAY?

What you need

Art paper in various colours, paints, brushes, scissors, felt-tipped pens, fabric scraps, wool, ribbon, glue, card, Blu-Tack, pieces of 'wood effect' wallpaper.

Preparation

Stick the art paper on a wall as a background for a nativity scene. Cut the wallpaper into strips.

What to do

Encourage the children to give you their ideas for making a group nativity scene for the wall. Let the children decide which people and animals should be in the scene and then create the people and animals by drawing, painting and collage. Stick the wallpaper strips here and there on the art paper to represent the back wall of a wooden stable. Cut out and arrange the people and animals in the picture and let the children make 'speech bubbles' from card

for them. Write down their suggestions for what the people are saying, and the sounds the animals make. Draw a 'bubble' around the words and let the children cut them out. Ask the children for their ideas for games which may be played with the 'speech bubbles' (for example one child makes an animal noise and another child has to find the appropriate 'bubble' and stick it on the picture with Blu-Tack).

Another idea is to put model animals in a bag. A child picks out an animal and must stick the appropriate 'bubble' by the animal.

Discussion

Do baby animals sound different from 'grown-up' animals? What do you think baby Jesus wanted when he cried or gurgled? What do you think the shepherds or the Three Wise Men said first when they arrived? What would Mary and Joseph have said to them?

This display relates mainly to the activity 'What did they say?' on page 16, but can also be used to stimulate discussion about 'Nativity rebus' on page 12, 'A long way' on page 14, 'Away in a manger' on page 15 and 'Smiling faces' on page 17.

CHRISTMAS PRESENTS

What you need

Frieze paper, white paper, paints, brushes, wool, fabric scraps, buttons, two tables, selection of Christmas gifts, gift catalogues, scissors, card, glue.

Preparation

Put one of the tables against a wall and attach the frieze paper behind and above it. On the other table arrange a selection of gifts (or pictures cut from catalogues and mounted on card). Make the gifts unisex, varied in size, appropriate for different ages and appealing to the senses.

What to do

Let the children decide on various kinds of people and pets to paint on the frieze paper (from the waist up), to look as though they are sitting behind the table. Include Father Christmas, a girl, a boy, a baby, a man, a woman and a pet. Add wool hair, fabric clothes, buttons and so on. Cut them out and stick them on the frieze paper.

Ask one child at a time to decide which gift to give to each character, and to say why. Emphasise that there are no 'right and wrong' choices. Ask the children for further ideas for gifts and characters.

Discussion

What presents did you give to people you know? How did you know what to give them? What did people give you? How did they know what to give you? Were any of the presents you received made 'by hand'? If you received any clothes, were they the right size? Did you receive any presents you could eat or smell? Did you especially like to touch any of your presents? Did any of your presents make a sound?

This display relates to the activities in Chapter 3 and the activities 'A present for Santa' on page 19 and 'The birds' Christmas Eve' on page 56.

frieze attached to wall

selection of gifts

CHRISTMAS VISITORS

What you need

A photocopier, photographs of children's families at Christmas time, frieze paper, sugar paper in various colours, felt-tipped pens, scissors, glue, Blu-Tack, adhesive tape.

Preparation

Cover a wall with frieze paper as a background for a display of the children's homes, which can be 'opened' to reveal photographs of the children's families inside. Just after the Christmas holiday, send a letter home asking for each child to bring one photograph of their family, showing relatives, friends, pets and so on at Christmas time.

What to do

Ask the children to each draw a picture of their homes on sugar paper, large enough to 'cover' their photograph. Let them draw windows, doors and so on with felt-tipped pens and then cut out their homes. Stick the photographs on the frieze paper and cover each one with the child's drawn picture. Stick these pictures down the left-hand side only with adhesive tape so that the picture can be opened like a book to reveal the photograph inside. Use a little Blu-Tack in the top right-hand corner of each home picture to ensure they stay flat. Ask one child at a time to choose a home and open it. The child whose home has been chosen can then talk about the photograph inside. Draw your own home, and bring in a photograph of your family to talk about too.

Discussion

Who visited you at Christmas? Can you count your visitors? What made you laugh, cry or be cross? Did babies or pets do anything you remember?

This display relates to the activities 'Christmas faces' on page 46 and 'Christmas visitors' on page 51.

frieze paper

children's drawings

child's family photograph

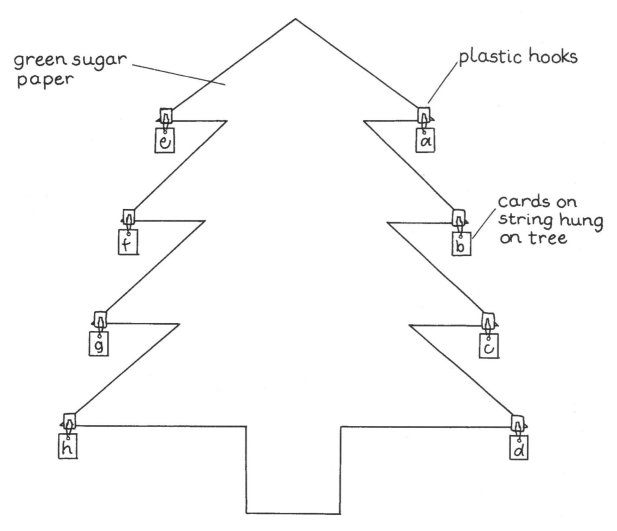

green sugar paper

plastic hooks

cards on string hung on tree

SPECIAL TREES

What you need

Green sugar paper, A1 sheet of card, glue, A4 sheet of card, felt-tipped pens, gift catalogues, scissors, glitter, a hole punch, string, adhesive tape, eight small 'peel off' plastic hooks.

Preparation

Cut out a Christmas tree from the green sugar paper and stick it on the card. Peel off the backing from the hooks and stick them on the tree. Cut the A4 card into pieces approximately 8cm x 8cm. Cut the string into pieces, each 25cm long.

What to do

Let the children decide what they would like to hang on a special tree. For example it could be all red things, different shapes, things to eat, things for a baby, a number or alphabet tree, a tree hung with tools, baking equipment or clothes. Ask the children to decide what to put on their trees and then to draw the items on the small cards or cut out pictures from catalogues. Show the children how to use a hole punch to make a hole in the top of the card and how to thread the string through. Help them tie a knot at the top so that their decorations can be hung on their special trees.

Discussion

Ask about the decorations on the children's trees at home. Ask if any are very old or if any can be eaten. Who chooses the decorations in the children's families? Who decorates the trees?

This display links with 'A tree from Norway' on page 58 and 'Martin's tree' on page 53.

CHAPTER 8
ASSEMBLIES

Opportunities to gather in a group to reflect are a vital part of Christmas celebrations. Specific ideas for Advent, Christmas around the world, as well as more general celebrations, are described here.

ADVENT

This gathering explores the theme of Advent (the word 'Advent' is taken from the Latin and means 'coming').

Advent marks the beginning of the liturgical year in many Christian communities and it is traditionally a time of anticipation and preparation for the celebrations of Christmas. The Advent period commences on the fourth Sunday before Christmas Day, and church services in December may include readings which focus on God's promise of a Saviour.

For many small children — whether or not they come from practising Christian homes — the word 'Advent' will probably evoke thoughts of calendars and chocolates! This gathering is designed to help them explore not only these commercial aspects of the pre-Christmas period, but also to reflect on its particular significance for Christmas.

Introduction

As the children enter the area, play some appropriate background music which reflects a mood of anticipation and excitement or invite some children to sing an Advent song.

Begin by encouraging the children to think of all the occasions to which they look forward with eagerness and excitement. Examples might include birthdays, holidays, trips to favourite locations, the visit of a much loved friend or relation or particular festivals and celebrations. In a small group, children may be able to give short, pre-planned presentations of some of their ideas, illustrated with pictures, drawings,

models or other suitable visual aids.

Encourage the children to spend a moment or two in thinking about the words they might use to describe their feelings as they look forward to events. They may suggest: excited, happy, impatient, thrilled, restless, unsettled, sleepless. Write these words out as captions or large signs.

Activity

On a table in the centre of the gathering, place an Advent ring or an Advent candle.

Talk to the children about Christmas and invite them to share their own feelings about this festival which is celebrated in a variety of ways, not just by Christians, but also by many other people. Lots of people, even if they are not religious, may well be caught up in a whirl of parties, shopping, cooking, decorations, cards and presents. Show pictures and artefacts to illustrate these examples.

Explain that for Christians, Advent is a time for thinking about the coming of Jesus into the world as a baby and for preparing to celebrate his birthday. Use the caption cards which express the children's feelings of anticipation to describe the way a Christian feels about Advent and Christmas.

Reflection

Darken the room as much as possible, and then light the Advent ring or the Advent candle. In silence, ask the children to close their eyes, or if they prefer, to watch the candle flame(s) and to think about the pleasure and excitement that waiting for a special event might bring.

Prayer

Choose a suitable prayer from a collection – Lion Publishing offers several for young children – and read this to the group. Some children may also be willing to read their own prayers about preparing to celebrate the birthday of Jesus.

Song

Conclude by inviting those children who wish to do so, to join in the singing of a song such as 'Christmas Giving on page 76.

AROUND THE WORLD

The focus for this gathering is on the many different ways of celebrating Christmas in a variety of cultural contexts.

Christians live and worship not only in this country, but also throughout the world. While they may share similar beliefs and celebrate the same festivals, they do so in ways which also reflect their own national and cultural identities and which draw on a wide range of traditions.

Introduce children to this diversity and encourage them to appreciate the many different ways in which Christian beliefs about Christmas are expressed.

Introduction

As the children enter the room, play some appropriate background music, based around the Christmas theme, but which is drawn from a variety of countries and cultures and from various periods of history. Contrast Gregorian chants with Gospel anthems or intersperse traditional German carols with calypso songs.

When the children have sat down, display standard images of Christmas celebrations in this country (greeting cards are a useful resource).

Invite the children to identify some of the many ways in which Christmas is celebrated in Britain and take care to emphasise some of the more familiar traditions, including turkey and plum pudding, Santa Claus, pantomimes, parties and carol-singing.

Activity

Show the children a large map of the world and ask one of them to come and find the UK. Make it clear that Christmas is celebrated in all parts of the country, not just in your own area.

Invite other children – who have been prepared for this task – to come and show other countries on the map which have some individual or distinctive Christmas traditions of their own. Examples might include the Netherlands and St Nicholas, Sweden and St Lucia, India and Christmas divas and so on.

Ask small groups of children to give a short presentation to depict some of these customs and traditions, particularly if they have some personal experience of them through their own families. Care must be taken to avoid stereotypes!

Reflection

As a focus for thought and reflection on the diversity of Christian practice, display some nativity images from around the world – many charities such as Christian Aid, Oxfam and CAFOD produce suitable Christmas cards.

While these are shown – one by one – invite the children to think about Christmas in these different countries as well as their own. Flags representing the countries featured could be held up as each one appears.

Prayer

Instead of a formal prayer, recite the words 'Happy Christmas' in as many different languages as possible, or say prayers which remember Christmas all over the world at this special time of year.

Song

End the gathering by inviting the children to sing some carols from around the world.

CELEBRATION SONG

The focus for this gathering is the book *Celebration Song* by James Berry and Louise Brierley (Puffin).

The book offers a new interpretation of the traditional Christmas story in the form of a lyrical and poignant poem. Mary, the mother of Jesus, is marking her son's first birthday, and while telling him of his past, she also wonders about his future. The book is illustrated with beautifully sensitive water-colours which present the main characters and their surroundings in a refreshingly different and original way.

Some children may also wish to relate the story to their own experiences, thinking not only of their pasts, but also their futures.

Introduction

As the children enter the area, play some Christmas music – popular, classical, traditional or perhaps with a Caribbean flavour to echo the illustrations in the book.

Remind the children that Christmas is a time when Christians join together to celebrate the birthday of Jesus.

Invite the children to share some of the ways in which they celebrate their own birthdays and those of their friends and families. Let them show pictures, paintings, drawings and models or act out scenes from parties in short dramas or role plays. Emphasise that birthdays are milestones; they are moments for reflection on the past and consideration of the future.

Activity

Read or tell the story 'Celebration Song', taking care that children are able to see the illustrations easily. Some children could even be prepared to act out the poem with appropriate props and costumes.

Reflection

As the story comes to an end, choose one favourite image from the story and display it clearly.

Invite the children to think carefully about the relationship between Jesus and Mary in the poem and to reflect on how he came into the world. Encourage them to consider what Mary might hope for her baby in the future.

Prayer

Conclude with a simple prayer which links with the closing verse of the poem. Invite those present to think of what is to be celebrated at Christmas, but also acknowledge what Christians may feel is wrong in the world.

Some children could light individual candles as a sign of their prayers for the future, stating what hope each candle represents.

Song

Draw the gathering to a close with listening to or singing a suitable hymn or carol, maybe one from this book, or play an appropriate piece of popular music such as 'Feed the World – Do They Know It's Christmas?' by Band Aid.

Collective worship in schools

The assemblies outlined here are suitable for use with children in nurseries and playgroups, but would need to be adapted for use with pupils at registered schools. As a result of legislation enacted in 1944, 1988 and 1993, there are now specific points to be observed when develping a programme of Collective Acts of Worship in a school.

Further guidance will be available from your local SACRE – Standing Advisory Council for RE.

POEMS AND ACTION RHYMES

LOOK AT THE BABY

'Look at the baby,' the oxen said,
'Lying so quiet in his soft straw bed.'
'Hope he's warm enough,' the donkey
sighed,
'It's awfully cold and dark outside.'
The lamb in the corner gave a bleat.
'Do you think he has enough to eat?'
The door of the stable opened wide.
Kings and shepherds came inside.
Kings and shepherds, angels too,
Crowding round for a better view.
The baby stirred, and looked, and smiled,
His mum and dad close by his side.
The old goat cried: 'He'll be alright,
He's surrounded by love in here
tonight!'

Margaret Willetts

ONE, TWO, THREE

One star
to guide them,
three gifts to lay
on the dusty stable floor, for
One Child in the hay.

One ox
to low there,
two donkeys to bray;
three wise men to gaze upon
One Child in the hay.

Judith Nicholls

BUSY, BUSY BETHLEHEM

Busy, busy Bethlehem,
People everywhere,
Busy, busy Bethlehem,
Not a bed to spare.

Pitter-patter donkey
Up to the stable door,
Pitter-patter donkey
On to the mat of straw.

Hush now, hush now Jesus,
Your life has just begun,
Hush now, hush now Jesus,
You are God's special one.

Coral Rumble

SANTA CLAUS ACTION RHYME

Here comes Santa in his sleigh,
high above the town.
(Fly one hand through the air, palm down.)

Look. He's found our chimney.
Now he's climbing down.
*(Bring hand to rest against upright other arm,
fist closed. This shows sledge parked up against
chimney. Show climbing down by using first two
fingers walking down upright arm.)*

He's picking out our presents
from his big and bulgy sack.
(Mime picking out presents from sack.)

Look. He's found our letter
and our special Christmas snack.
*(Look at open palm to show letter. Mime
nibbling a mince pie for snack.)*

Now he's climbing up again
to get back in his sleigh.
*(Show two fingers climbing back up upright
forearm. Show sleigh as open hand, palm down,
ready to go.)*

'Ho, ho, ho!' says Santa
as he hurries on his way.
*(Call 'Ho, ho, ho!' from cupped hands. Then
show hurrying away with hand as sleigh again,
moving through air, palm downward.)*

Tony Mitton

QUESTIONS ON CHRISTMAS EVE

In the night sky, far away
Is that Santa with his sleigh?

On my rooftop, what's that noise?
Is it Santa with some toys?

Down the chimney, will he creep
When he things I'm fast asleep?

In my bedroom, will I hear
Someone tiptoe very near?

In the darkness, what's that shape?
Is it Santa's hat and cape?

In the morning, will there be
Lots of presents — just for me?

Trevor Harvey

JESUS

Christmas is for Jesus.
It's His birthday, you see.
So I'm very lucky
That He shares it with me.

Barbara Garrad

CHRISTMAS COOKIES

Stir a little mixture,
Shake a little spice,
Stick a little finger in,
Suck it if it's nice!
Cutters at the ready!
Give the dough a roll,
Bake the cookie bells and stars,
Make a little hole,
Cool them on a wire rack —
Safe to ice them now —
Thread a coloured ribbon through,
Hang them on a bough!

Sue Cowling

OUR CHRISTMAS CARDS

Mum's put out crayons,
paints and card
and now we're drawing,
thinking hard,
painting and colouring
Christmasy things —
a snowman, Santa Claus,
Christmas trees, kings.
I'm making cards
for Granny and Bill.
Tom's done a card
for Auntie Jill.
Inside we write
'Merry Christmas'
and 'Love'
and Mum gives us
pretty stamps with a dove.
Mum writes the address
on the envelope, so
our Christmas cards
are ready to go.

Penny Kent

WHAT'S IN THE PARCEL?

Lift it, sniff it,
rattle, shake!
Is it heavy?
Will it break?

Tear the corner,
listen, look!
Scooter? Computer?
Adventure book?

Can I bend it, throw it,
spend it, lick it?
Will it fly?
Or could I kick it?

Will it work outside?
In rain?
A skateboard? Bike?
Electric train?

Here we go ...
Oh, NO!
Not SOCKS AGAIN!

Judith Nicholls

A THINKING CHRISTMAS

A turkey dinner
at Christmas is great!
THINK
Somewhere…a boy
with an empty plate.

The Christmas tree lights
shine red, green, and gold.
THINK
Somewhere…a girl
shivering and cold.

Presents and parties!
Yes, that's Christmas Day!
THINK
Somewhere…a child
asleep in the hay.

Wes Magee

CHRISTMAS MYSTERY

Where is the pudding that Santa made,
the one he made himself,
the one he soaked in brandy
and left to stand on the shelf?

The one he filled with raisins
and sugar and suet and fruit,
which stood so sweet and tempting,
the one he called, 'A beaut!'

The one that he was going to serve
with rich rum-butter and cream,
the one so dark and shiny,
the one he called, 'A dream!'

Where is the pudding that Santa made?
It seems to have disappeared.
And why does he doze with a smile on his
face
and raisins in his beard?

Tony Mitton

WAVE YOUR HANDS FOR CHRISTMAS!

Wave your hands for Christmas!
Stretch your arms up high
If you should see a reindeer
Careering through the sky!

Rub your hands for Christmas,
Picture the array
Of toys and books and games and sweets
On Santa Claus's sleigh!

Clap your hands for Christmas!
Thank the man in red
Who filled the Christmas stocking
At the bottom of your bed!

Lend a hand for Christmas!
Spend an hour or two
On somebody who isn't
As fortunate as you!

Sue Cowling

THE CHRISTMAS TREE LIGHTS

There are twenty
brand-new Christmas lights
draped around
        our Christmas tree.
They are a very
    special gift
    that Gran has
        sent to me.

Each little light
is star-shaped.
Switch them on
    — oh, what a sight!
There's a brand-new
    constellation
    shining brightly
        in the night!

Wes Magee

IS IT COLD AT CHRISTMAS?

Is it cold at Christmas
Full of ice and snow?
Are there frosty windows
Do the fires glow?

Other children's countries
Wake up to the sun
Barbecues and beaches
Start the Christmas fun

Other children's countries
Bitter cold and grey
Wrap in furry hats and coats
Upon Christmas Day

Other children's countries
Always dark, and night
Huddle in their cabins
Where the fire is bright

Is it cold at Christmas?
Not if we keep warm
With our strong brick houses
To keep away the storm

Maureen Warner

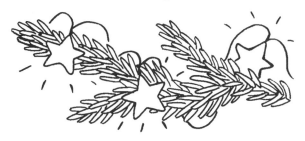

SUNNY SANTA

Down under in Australia
(so they say)
Santa puts a sun-umbrella
on his sleigh.

He rides along in sandals
and shorts of red,
with a big straw sunhat
on his head.

But isn't he cold
in the ice and snow?

Not in sunny Australia,
NO!

Tony Mitton

SONGS

THERE ISN'T ANY ROOM

C   G   C

There's no room at the inn to-night. The rooms are full and the door's shut tight.

G   C

1. There's no-where you can rest to-night. There is-n't an-y room at the inn.
2. Just the sta-ble if that's al-right. There is-n't an-y room at the inn.

Clive Barnwell

THE GREATEST GIFT

Slowly

Dm   **Am**   **Dm**   **Am**   **B♭**   **C**   **F**

1. Snug - gled in the hay,   ve - ry far a - way,   Ba - by Je - sus lay at Christ - mas.
2. An - gels filled the air   round the sta - ble where   Ba - by Je - sus lay at Christ - mas.

Dm   **Am**   **Dm**   **Am**   **B♭**   **C**   **F**

Un - der - neath the bright   star that shone to light   Ba - by Je - sus there at Christ - mas.
Shep - herds went to see,   on their bend - ed knee,   Ba - by Je - sus there at Christ - mas.

Chorus

B♭   **C**   **F**   **B♭**   **F**   **C**   **Dm**

What a gift, oh, what a gift, oh, what a gift to give us.

B♭   **C**   **F**   **B♭**   **F**   **C**   **F**

What a gift, oh, what a gift, the great - est gift of Christ - mas.

Clive Barnwell

PHOTOCOPIABLE RESOURCES

SANTA, SANTA

Not too fast

1. San - ta, San - ta with his beard so white,
Hur - ries o - ver roof - tops on Christ - mas Night.

Play 3 times

Slower

2. Rudolf, Rudolf with his nose so red,
Helps to pull the sleigh when we're
All in bed.

3. Silver sleigh that never makes a noise,
Loaded up with gifts for the
Girls and boys.

Susan Eames

FATHER CHRISTMAS MAKES THE TOYS

Quite fast

1. Fath - er Christ - mas makes the toys, makes the toys, makes the toys, Gives them out to the girls and boys for Christ - mas day. With a tap tap tap, and a great big twist, He makes all the toys on the Christ - mas list.

2. Father Christmas makes the toys,
Makes the toys, makes the toys,
Gives them out to the girls and boys for Christmas Day.
With a click, click, click, and a great big twist,
He makes all the toys on the Christmas list,
PLAY ON CLAVES: Click click click, click click click,
click click click click, click.

3. With a shake, shake, shake…
(PLAY SHAKERS)

4. With a ding, ding, ding…
(PLAY BELLS)

5. With a clonk, clonk, clonk…
(PLAY TAMBOURINES)

Invent other verses if you want, and always have a distinctive percussive sound
on the 'great big twist'.

Ann Bryant

CHRISTMAS GIVING

Gently

| C | Am7 | Dm7 | G7 | C | Am7 | Dm7 | G7 |

Christ - mas giv - ing,___ Christ - mas liv - ing, A time for peace and joy.

| .C | Am7 | Dm7 | G7 | C | G7 | C *Fine* C7 |

Christ - mas giv - ing,___ Christ - mas liv - ing For ev' - ry girl and boy. I will

| F | G7 | Em | A7 | Dm7 | G7 | C | C7 |

make some cards for my mum and dad, My friends and fam - i - ly. It's a

D.C. al Fine

| F | G7 | Em | A7 | D | D7 | G | G7 |

time for hap - pi - ness to be had for ev' - ry - one to see.

Johanne Levy

CHRISTMAS PUD

What goes in to make the Christ-mas Pud? What goes in to make it taste so good?

1. Cur-rants,___ rais-ins,___ ap-ple,___ spice, That's what makes our Pud so good, good, good!
2. Su-et,___ le-mon,___ just the___ rind,
3. Flo-ur,___ su-gar,___ bread-crumbs,___ eggs,

4. Mix it, stir it, cook it, then
You'll know why our Pud's so good, good, good!

This can develop into a cumulative song.
Add more ingredients each time it is sung ie
1st time — currants, raisins, apple, spice,
2nd time — add suet, lemon, just the rind etc
so that on the 4th time, you should have a delicious Christmas pud!

Peter Morrell

CHRISTMAS CHEER

Chorus

Hel - lo Christ - mas Tree, Wait - ing for us here. We will de - co - rate your branch - es

For our Christ - mas cheer. 1. Hang some glit - ter and a bell, String some fair - y lights as well.

1,2 etc. **Last time** *D.C. al Coda*

Coda

Christ - mas time is here.

> **2.** Put some tinsel all around
> And some presents to be found.
> Chorus: Hello, Christmas Tree

✧ Make up some more verses.
✧ Singing game: make a circle round a pretend (or real) tree. The children hold hands while they walk round the tree singing the chorus. They stop to mime
the verses.
Add percussion, choosing contrasting sounds:
For example
Chorus: tambourine / tambour / bongo drum
Verse: triangle / bells / shaker

Jean Gilbert

PAPER CHAINS

Sing unaccompanied

Pap - er chains of red and yel - low, Pap - er chains of red and yel - low,

Pap - er chains of red and yel - low, Hang them from the ceil - ing.

Tune: Trad (Bobby Shaftoe)

Actions: during the first three lines of the song the children make 'loops' of the first finger and thumb on both hands, intertwined to make two paper chain links. (They could also do it with the child sitting next to them in the circle.) The finger links are opened and closed while they sing.

On the last line they point index fingers at two ceiling corners and move them together showing the shape of the chain.

To change colours: either allow children to choose partner colours for the song or — have cards (coloured or named) face down in the circle and the chosen child turns two face up.

Sue Nicholls

SHARING CHRISTMAS

Lilting

D

We'll share our Christ-mas with all of the world, We'll share our Christ-mas with boys and with girls.

Em   **A**   **D**

1. Wheth-er you live where it's hot or it's cold, Wheth-er you're young, or wheth-er you're old, We'll
2. Wheth-er you're near or you live far a-way, Wheth-er it's night or wheth-er it's day, We'll
3. Wheth-er you're hap-py or wheth-er you're sad, We'll send God's love and then you'll be glad, We're

1,2.   **Em**   **A**   **D**   **3.**   **Em**   **A**   **D**

share our Christ-mas with you.   shar-ing our Christ-mas with you.
share our Christ-mas with you.

Happy
Christmas!

> 2. Whether you're near or you live far away,
>   Whether it's night or whether it's day.
>
> 3. Whether you're happy or whether you're sad,
>   We'll send God's love and then you'll be glad,
>   We're sharing our Christmas with you.
>   Happy Christmas!

Peter Morrell

STORIES

THE STORY OF ST NICHOLAS

A long time ago, in a country which we now call Turkey, there was a man called Nicholas. He was a rich man and very kind. One day Nicholas decided to go for a walk. He put on his fine and fancy cloak and off he went. As he was walking, he saw a man sitting by the roadside looking very sad. The man was not wearing a cloak. Instead he was huddled inside an old, patched blanket. Nicholas walked up to the man and said 'You look very sad. What is the matter?' The poor man replied, 'I am a very poor man. I have three daughters and no money to buy any food. This morning we looked in the cupboards in our little house, and there was no food at all. I do not know what to do.'

Nicholas decided that he would like to give the family some money but instead of just giving the poor man some money Nicholas thought it would also be kind to do it in secret, so that it would be a wonderful surprise for the family. Nicholas said to the poor man, 'I have to go now, but try not to be too sad because I think that soon there might be a big surprise for you! Good bye!'

The poor man went home and found his daughters washing their stockings in the wash tub and hanging them to dry on a washing line across the fireplace. Each daughter hung up a pair of stockings — one, two; three four; five, six — six stockings altogether. That night when everyone was fast asleep, Nicholas carefully and quietly climbed on to the family's roof. Then he put his hand in his pocket, and brought out six golden coins. Carefully he dropped them down the chimney one at a time, so that each one fell inside a stocking — plop, plop, plop, plop, plop, plop! The next morning, when the daughters went to get their stockings, they were amazed and delighted to find the coins inside! This happened on the next night, too, and the night after that. Nicholas dropped money into the daughters' stockings for three nights so that in the end, the family had a lot of money to buy food. The girls' father often wondered whether the rich man in the fine and fancy cloak had dropped the money down the chimney, but he never found out for sure.

Nicholas carried on being very kind to poor people. After he died, everyone decided he should be called Saint Nicholas. A Saint is a very kind person. People in Holland called him Saint Nikolaas, and later this name changed to Sinterklaas or Santa Claus, and also Father Christmas.

Linda Mort and Janet Morris

THE STORY OF THE FIRST CHRISTMAS

Joseph gave one last look around the house before leaving. Everything was neat and tidy, and well swept, ready for them for when they got back. He hoped he hadn't forgotten anything, because he knew they would be away for quite a few days. He tightened up the straps around the bundles on the back of the donkey, and taking the rope tied to the halter, he led Mary and the donkey out onto the narrow track which led through the hills near to Nazareth.

'It's a pity we have to make this journey now,' he thought. Mary would be having the baby soon, and it was a long way for her to travel. She should really be resting. But it was no use arguing, everyone had to go to Bethlehem to sign the register, so they had best get there as soon as they could. At least there would be lots of other people on the journey, so there would be less chance of robbers suddenly turning up! 'The more of us the better,' he thought.

He began to change his mind as they drew near Bethlehem. There were so many people on the road. Merchants selling bread and fruit to the travellers met them on the last stage of the journey. Although she didn't complain, he could see that Mary was very tired now. They were both looking forward to having some supper and settling down to a good night's sleep.

But the streets of Bethlehem were packed. It had been useful having company on the roads, but now they were being pushed and shoved by the crowds of people milling around the tiny streets. People had come from villages for miles around.

'Won't be long now Mary,' said Joseph, 'I'll soon find us a place to stay.' But in fact, Joseph found that it wasn't going to be easy at all. Everywhere was full up. Round and round the town he went calling at every guesthouse and inn asking for a bed for the night.

As it started to get dark, Mary bent and whispered to Joseph. 'I shall have to lie down soon, I think the baby is coming.' Poor Joseph, he was so tired himself, he had tried just about everywhere, and now he was even more worried about Mary. He turned down a small passageway leading out of the village back to the hills. Outside a tiny inn, the innkeeper was just taking a last look around before locking up.

'Do you by any chance have any spare room for the night?' asked Joseph desperately.

As the innkeeper began to shake his head, Joseph said quickly, 'No-one has any room. Our baby is due, and anywhere would be better than going back into the hills.'

'You're right there,' said the innkeeper, 'too many robbers around.' He looked thoughtful. 'I tell you what,' he said, rubbing his beard, 'I really don't have any room, we're absolutely full, but I do have a stable at the back, if you don't mind sharing with the animals.'

As Joseph hesitated, the man went on, 'At least it's warm and dry, and a bale of straw will make a comfortable bed.'

'Thank you,' said Joseph. 'That's very kind of you.'

As he made Mary comfortable, Joseph looked around the stable at the innkeeper's oxen, and his own donkey. 'It seems a strange place for a special baby to be born in,' he thought. Some months before, an angel had spoken to him in a dream, telling him that Mary's baby was the Son of God, and that he must take care of her. Now, he wondered why God had chosen such a simple place for the birth.

During the night, the baby was born, and Joseph called him Jesus.

Soon afterwards, Joseph heard people whispering outside, and he got up to see who was there. Shepherds were standing shyly outside the stable, each carrying a small lamb.

'Something wonderful happened to us tonight, whilst we were sleeping by our sheep on the hills near Bethlehem,' one of them said, 'A blinding light woke us up, and an angel told us to take gifts to a special baby. We followed a bright star, and it stopped right above this stable. May we see the baby King please, and give him our lambs. These are the only gifts we have, for we are poor shepherds and do not have much money.'

Retold by Brenda Williams

Joseph felt very proud as he led the shepherds inside, and showed them the baby Jesus.

Very soon, the innkeeper came running in. 'Who is this child?' he asked. Three kings dressed in rich robes, and riding on camels have arrived in Bethlehem and demand to see the baby. They say he is the King of Kings!' The poor man looked very flustered. 'How can I have refused a room to such a special baby?' he said. 'He should have been born in a palace.'

Joseph smiled. 'You did more for us than anyone else, and I am sure this is the way God planned it.'

When the kings arrived, they too were surprised at the simple surroundings, but they knew it was the right place, because they had followed the star for many years from the East, and now it had stopped right above the stable.

Because they were rich, they were able to bring expensive oils of frankincense and myrrh to make the room smell lovely. And they gave him gold too. They knelt beside him and knew that their long journey was over. They had found the King they had been waiting for.

A BUSY TIME FOR MRS CHRISTMAS

Mrs Christmas didn't know what to do! Ever since breakfast all she could hear was 'Atishoo! Atishoo! Oh dear! What shall I do?' She looked across the room at the big armchair. There sat Father Christmas wrapped in a blanket, hugging a hot water bottle. It seemed like he had been sneezing and moaning for hours. She had fetched mugs of hot lemon drink sweetened with honey, filled the hot water bottle when it got cold, and handed

out lots of tissues but Father Christmas's cold was definitely getting worse. 'Whatever shall I do tonight?' said Father Christmas. 'All the children will be expecting me — it's Christmas Eve, I can't let them down.'

Mrs Christmas shook her head. 'Well if you are as poorly as you are now I can't see how you can make the trip. The children will just have to wait until you're better. You've never been late before.

Father Christmas shook his head. 'Christmas Eve and no presents — but what will they do on Christmas Day? How will they spend the day? They'll think I've forgotten them — and never believe I'll come again. Atishoo! Atishoooooo!'

Mrs Christmas didn't know what to say. Everybody had worked so hard to get things ready. The toys were sorted and put into sacks. Labels were written and parcels all wrapped. The reindeer were resting, their harness all ready and as for the sledge — it gleamed with the polish. Rudolph was leading — his nose shining bright. Oh what a disaster to happen tonight!

'Try and have a rest now. We'll just have to see how you feel a bit later,' said Mrs Christmas. 'I've just got a few more jobs to do and everything will be ready for our Christmas dinner too.'

As Mrs Christmas baked her mince pies and put the red robin on the Christmas cake she had an idea. 'Well — I've never done it before but I've heard about it so many times I'm sure I could do it', she said to herself. 'If Father Christmas is no better by teatime that's what I'll do!'

The cuckoo popped out of the clock to say it was five o'clock. Mrs Christmas looked up and listened. What was that noise? A strange growling noise was coming out of the room. She hurried out of the kitchen and peeped around the door. 'ZZZZZzzzzzzzz, Zzzzzzzzz.' It wasn't an animal, it was Father Christmas fast asleep.

'Well that settles it,' said Mrs Christmas with a smile. 'I'm not going to wake him up now he's asleep. He isn't fit to go out tonight in the cold. He'll go and get the flu next.' She went into the kitchen and made a big flask of coffee. She cut some bread and made some jam sandwiches. The she gathered together some crisps, and fruit and a little bar of chocolate. She opened the hall cupboard and took out a big pair of boots, a long red coat and a red hat with a white furry pom pom. As she crept out of the door she picked up the A-Z of the World, a thick address book and a pair of black gloves.

Harry was fast asleep. His empty sack was hanging over the bottom of the bed. All sorts of things were whirling around in his head — fire engines and farm yard animals, computer games and new trainers. Slowly the door opened and somebody all in red was filling his sack with presents. Crash! — a shiny red tractor fell to the floor. 'Oh bother!' whispered a voice. Harry woke up and rubbed his eyes. At the bottom of his bed he saw Father Christmas bending down. But what was that — as Father Christmas turned to go he saw a pair of earrings shaped liked cats and a soft gentle voice whispered 'Happy Christmas Harry — have a nice day.' A black finger moved towards a bright red mouth and someone said 'Shh — our secret' as she moved away.

Anne Farr

BABOUSHKA – A CHRISTMAS STORY FROM RUSSIA

Once upon a time there lived a little old lady called Baboushka. She lived all alone in a little cottage in the woods a long way out of town. She did not have many visitors, but she never felt lonely. She loved to stay at home, cleaning and polishing, cooking and sewing, knitting and looking after the animals.

One cold winter's evening, as she sat knitting by the fire, she heard a sound outside. She stopped knitting to listen.

'I hear footsteps on my path,' she said. 'Who can that be at this time of night?'

There was a gentle tap on the door.

'Who's there?' Baboushka called as she opened the door a crack. She could see three tall men standing on the doorstep.

'Kind lady,' said one, 'may we come in and rest? We've travelled such a long way and we're very tired.'

Baboushka opened the door a little wider.

'My name is Caspar,' said the man, 'and my friends are Melchior and Balthazar. We're searching for the new Baby King.'

'I've no baby here,' said Baboushka, 'nor a king, for that matter, but you're welcome to come in. You can share my supper and you may rest on my spare beds.'

As Caspar, Melchior and Balthazar stepped into her house, Baboushka gasped. They were dressed in the finest robes she had ever seen, threaded with gold and silver. Jewels of every colour of the rainbow shone in the flickering candle light.

These men must be kings, she thought as she fed them soup from her pan and bread from her oven.

'Tell me about this Baby King you're seeking,' she said.

'We've seen a bright new star in the sky,' said Melchior.

'It means that the Christ Child has been born,' said Caspar. 'He's born to be the King of Kings.'

'We're following the star,' said Balthazar, 'until it leads us to the new Baby King.'

'We'll kneel down before Him and offer Him our gifts,' said Caspar.

They showed Baboushka the presents they had brought. When they had finished their supper, they lay down on the beds and fell fast asleep. When they had rested, Baboushka gave them more food and then showed them the way back to the road.

'Thank you for your kindness,' said Caspar.

'Why don't you come with us?' said Melchior.

'I would love to come,' said Baboushka, 'but I have so much work to do. I must find a few presents to give to the Baby King. Then I'll follow you.'

'Be as quick as you can,' said Caspar.

'I'll catch up with you as soon as I've finished my chores,' said Baboushka.

When they had gone, Baboushka washed the dishes and cleaned the house. Then she went to her cupboard and found some old toys to take to the Baby King.

'Oh dear,' she said. 'These are broken and dirty. I must mend them and wash them before I go.'

At last she was ready. Carrying a large bag of toys, she set off after the three kings, but she had taken too long getting ready and however fast she travelled, she could not catch up with them. Fresh snow had fallen and covered their footprints. She did not know which way they had gone.

'Oh, well,' she said. 'I will have to find the Baby on my own.'

Day after day, Baboushka hurried on in search of the new Baby King.

'Have you seen three kings pass this way?' she asked a farmer.

'Kings don't come to these parts,' laughed the farmer.

'Have you seen a bright star in the sky?' she asked the traveller.

'There's millions of stars up there,' laughed the traveller.

'Have you seen the new Baby King?' she asked a shepherd.

'There's always babies being born,' laughed the shepherd,' but none of them is a king.'

Baboushka was very sad. She wanted so much to find the Baby King. She wandered to many more places, asking about the Christ Child, but nobody knew where she could find Him. As she travelled, she came across many babies and children. Some of them were ill. Some of them were unhappy. So she gave them each a toy.

'I will leave a present at all the houses,' she said to herself, 'in case the Christ Child is there.'

Ever since then, Baboushka has travelled all over the country, looking for the Christ Child. She has never found Him yet, but every year, twelve days after Christmas, she leaves gifts for all the children, just in case.

Jill Atkins

MOLE'S BEST CHRISTMAS

Mole liked the best of everything. He lived in the biggest house in the wood, wore the smartest clothes and thought he was much better than everyone else.

'This year,' he decided, 'I'm going to have the best Christmas ever. I'm going to have the biggest Christmas tree I can find, hundreds of presents and as much food as I can eat.'

So, he bought a great big tree, decorated it with lots of pretty baubles and tinsel and stood it in the middle of the room. Then he went shopping and bought himself lots of presents.

'This is definitely going to be the best Christmas ever,' Mole thought happily as he wrapped up the presents and put them around the tree.

As soon as Mole woke up on Christmas morning, he scrambled out of bed to see what Santa Claus had left in the giant-sized stocking he had hung at the end of his bed. At first he thought the stocking was empty then he found a small parcel tucked into the toe. Quickly, he pulled it out and ripped it open. Mole just couldn't believe what he found inside – a packet of party invitations! He rubbed his eyes and stared at it in disbelief.

Party invitations! What sort of present was that? Mole threw the packet down on his bed and stamped downstairs very crossly. Well, he didn't need Santa's present. He had lots by the tree.

But it wasn't much fun unwrapping those presents, he already knew what was inside. Mole left most of them unwrapped

and walked grumpily over to the window. Rabbit was walking past on his way to Squirrel's house, carrying a present under his arm.

'Hey, Rabbit!' called Mole. 'What did Santa bring you for Christmas?'

'Some chocolate and a trumpet and a book and a big ball!' smiled Rabbit. 'What did he bring you?'

'Oh, twice as much as that!' said Mole and he shut the window crossly. Humph! All that for Rabbit and all he got was a packet of party invitations! Still, who cared? He had the biggest Christmas tree, the most Christmas presents and a cupboard full of delicious food. He was having the best Christmas ever.

Mole put on his party hat and sat down to eat his Christmas dinner. But suddenly he didn't feel hungry anymore. Christmas wasn't much fun when you had no one to talk to, pull crackers with or play games with.

He went over to the window and looked out. Squirrel and Hedgehog were walking past, talking and laughing together. Mole watched as they went to knock on Rabbit's door. Rabbit opened the door, smiled and let them in. Mole watched them sadly. He wished he had some friends to enjoy Christmas with.

Suddenly, he had an idea. He went upstairs and picked up Santa's present off the floor.

He carefully took out each party invitation and wrote 'Please come to Mole's Christmas party at 4 o'clock today'. Then he went out and delivered them.

For the next few hours Mole was very busy. He wrapped up a present each for all the other animals and put them by the tree. Then he laid the table with food and crackers and party hats.

At four o'clock there was a knock at the door. Mole went to open it and there were Rabbit, Squirrel, Hedgehog, Badger and all the other animals, all looking rather surprised.

'Merry Christmas, Mole!' they all said. 'Thank you for inviting us to your party.'

'Come in! Come in!' smiled Mole. 'There are presents for everyone and plenty to eat and drink.'

What a brilliant time they all had! The dancing and singing went on all evening, and when all the animals finally left they all declared that it was the best party ever.

Much later that night, a very tired but happy Mole went to bed. This was definitely the best Christmas he had ever had, he thought happily, and it was all thanks to Santa and his party invitations. Without them he would never have learnt how much fun it was to give presents to his friends and share things with them. From now on he was going to be a different and much happier Mole.

Karen King

THEMES
for early years

Smiling faces

Cut out and stick on faces for Mary, Joseph, baby Jesus and the Three Wise Men. Stick on fabric pieces to decorate their clothes.

THEMES
for early years

Make a mobile for a baby

THEMES
for early years

Christmas gifts

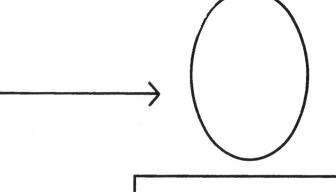

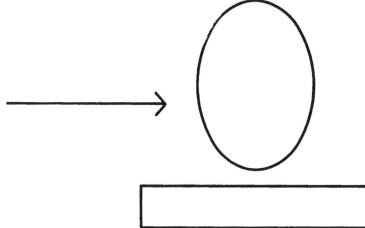

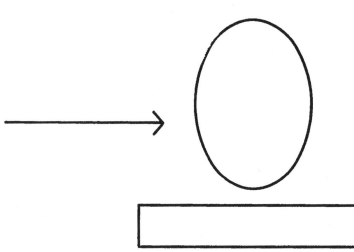

THEMES
for early years

On Christmas night

THEMES
for early years

Dressing Santa

Follow this key to colour in Santa's clothes.

If you throw 1 colour in his hat, 2 = jacket; 3 = belt; 4 = trousers; 5 = wellingtons; 6 = gloves.

Set the table

Can you lay the table ready for Christmas dinner?
Each bear needs a mat, a plate, a napkin, a cracker,
a knife, fork and spoon and a glass.

THEMES
for early years

By day and by night

THEMES
for early years

Feed the pets

Draw a line to show which pet eats which food.

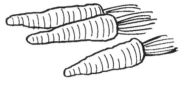

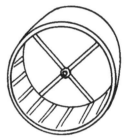

RECOMMENDED MATERIALS

NATIVITY STORY BOOKS
A Christmas Story Brian Wildsmith (Oxford University Press)
The Christmas Story Sheila Moxley (Tango Books)
The Christmas Story Nicola Smee (Orchard Books)
The Christmas Story Anne Civardi (Puffin)
The Story of Christmas Anita Ganeri (Dorling Kindersley)
The Story of Christmas Jane Ray (Orchard Books)

STORY BOOKS
Arthur's Christmas Marc Brown (Red Fox)
Elmer in the Snow David McKee (Red Fox)
Harry and the Snow King Ian Whybrow (Levinson Books)
The Jolly Christmas Postman Janet and Alan Ahlberg (Heinemann)
Kipper's Snowy Day Mick Inkpen (Hodder Children's Books)
Little Bear's Christmas Norbert Landa (Bloomsbury Children's Books)
The Little Reindeer Michael Foreman (Anderson Press)
Mog's Christmas Judith Kerr (Collins Picture Lions)
The Night Before Christmas Clement C Moore (Oxford University Press)
Olive, the other reindeer J Otto Seibold and Vivian Walsh (Chronicle Books)
Sssh! Julie Sykes (Magi Books)
The Snowman Raymond Briggs (Picture Puffin)
The Snow Tree Caroline Repchuk (Templar Publishing)

Spot's First Christmas Eric Hill (Picture Puffin)
Teddy's Christmas Peter Bowman (Tango Books)
This is the Star Joyce Dunbar (Doubleday)

INFORMATION BOOKS
A to Z Christmas Beverley Mathias and Ruth Thomson (Watts Books)
The Children's Illustrated Bible Stories retold by Selina Hastings (Dorling Kindersley)
Celebration Barnabus and Anabel Kindersley (Dorling Kindersley)
Bright Ideas for Early Years: Christmas Activities Susan Godfrey (Scholastic)
The Christmas Almanac Michael Stephenson (OUP)
A Christmas Stocking Louise Betts Egan (Simon and Schuster)
Bright Ideas for Early Years: Festivals and Celebrations Rhona Whiteford and Jim Fitzsimmons (Scholastic)

SONGS AND POEMS
'Bright Star Shining – Poem for Christmas' selected by Michael Harrison and Christopher Stuart Clark (Oxford University Press)
Festivals Carole Court (Scholastic Collections)
'Christmas Tinderbox' (A and C Black)
'Ding Dong Merrily on High' Francesca Crespi (Frances Lincoln)

OTHER RESOURCES
Advent Calendar felt wall hanging, available from Step by Step Ltd.
Emotions Glove Puppets, available from Galt Educational.
3D Felt Nativity Set, available from Step by Step Ltd.
Nativity stand-up inset puzzle, available from Step by Step Ltd.
Santa's house wooden inset puzzle, available from Step by Step Ltd.
Advent rings and candles are available from Articles of Faith.

USEFUL ADDRESSES
Step by Step Ltd, Lavenham Road, Beeches Trading Estate, Yate, Bristol, BS37 5QX.
Galt-Educational, Culvert Street, Oldham, Lancashire.
Articles of Faith. Resource House, Kay Street, Bury, Lancashire BL9 6BU.

PHOTOCOPIABLE RESOURCES